LIVE MORE

WORK

BETTER

LIVE

MORE

A Practical Guide to a Balanced Life

WORK

BETTER

Gayle Hilgendorff

BASCOM HILL
PUBLISHING GROUP

BASCOM HILL
PUBLISHING GROUP

Bascom Hill Publishing Group
322 First Avenue N, 5th floor
Minneapolis, MN 55401
612.455.2294
www.bascomhillbooks.com

The diet and exercise tips offered in this book are for educational and informational purposes only and may not be construed as medical advice. The information is not intended to replace medical advice offered by physicians.

If you are interested in knowing more about my Executive Health and Leadership Coaching work, please feel free to visit me here: www.thehealthyleader.com.

ISBN-13: 978-1-63413-356-2
LCCN: 2015902727

Distributed by Itasca Books

Cover Design by Alan Pranke
Typeset by James Arneson
Edited for Bascom Hill by Robert Christian Schmidt

Printed in the United States of America

Thank you, Dad – for giving me masculine strength.

Thank you, Mom – for giving me feminine strength.

Most of all, thank you, RJ – You are why I love living.

CONTENTS

Introduction

My own life-rebalancing act was driven by my desire to have the unimaginable—a successful career—without forfeiting my life, health, or relationships.

My career was everything I wanted it to be. I was on the "fast track" to partnership at a consulting company. I made more money than I had ever thought possible, with the promise that the higher I climbed up the corporate ladder, the more I would make. I enjoyed my job. I enjoyed my career. I enjoyed my success.

The year I was nominated for partnership was the hardest year I've ever lived. I was someone who gave 150% to everything I did and a promotion to partner was the biggest thing I had ever done. It required more effort, time, and work. I took on additional responsibilities. I worked nights and weekends. I gave my supervisor and colleagues every bit of my energy, time, and focus. But I was unhappy—and unhealthy.

I enjoy being outdoors, especially hiking in the woods or relaxing on a beach. I married my high school sweetheart because we're best friends, soul mates, and I can't imagine my life without him. I enjoy eating and cooking healthy food, and appreciate how I look and feel when I do. I believe that we are put on this earth to serve a purpose and leave things better than we found them. I believe in miracles and I believe in a universal power that wants us to be happy, loved, and free to live our lives as we choose.

I was unable to live up to any of those ideals the year I was nominated for partnership. I was up at 5:00 a.m. every morning because it was just easier to get up and start my day than it was to lie in bed and pretend I was sleeping when, in reality, I could feel every cell of my body vibrating with stress. After way too much coffee and way too little food, I would find myself craving a cigarette. No, I wasn't a smoker at all, but I envied my friends who did smoke; after all, they got to go outside for a ten-minute break every few hours. Usually a healthy eater, I went from feeling good about what I put in my mouth to justifying fast food and alcohol as a "well-deserved end of a long day."

Too much fast food and alcohol inevitably impacted my mood, and those few minutes I got to spend with my husband each night usually ended in me either falling asleep on the couch or yelling at him for something I wouldn't even remember the next day. But every day was the same. I was addicted to higher and higher performance. I was determined to prove that I could handle the pressure. I overcommitted myself and overpromised my time, attention, and energy. The more I could get done, the better I thought my chances would be for success. The harder I worked, the less chance of failure. I figured that once I got to my ultimate goal of promotion, life would be better. So why not ignore my life for a while knowing that *someday* I could make it all back up?

The truth is, in my mind, getting that promotion would have meant that I had finally been successful in life. My parents could brag about me to their friends. My husband would be proud to introduce me to coworkers. Friends would *ooh* and *ahh* over my new car and new clothes or the latest business trip, because I was a big corporate executive. Being promoted meant that other people would acknowledge that I deserved to earn money and speak at meetings — and my opinions would matter. Without the promotion, I was just a hard worker who simply wasn't good enough.

I was passed up for the promotion. Whether it was the anger or bewilderment that rendered me speechless, I'll never really know. All I knew was that my entire life for the previous year had apparently been a complete waste. I wanted to crawl through the phone line that separated me from my boss and strangle her. But then a strange thing happened.

I always have the radio turned on. I love music. Over the years, I have discovered how music can comfort, inspire, energize, and enlighten me. I received the phone call informing me of my "no promotion" situation while I was at home on a Friday afternoon, preparing for a celebratory glass of champagne. The radio was on, but I had turned it down for the call. When I got off the phone, I turned it up as loud as I could. I wanted to fade away into the music. As I sat on the couch planning exactly how I would get my revenge, a song came on the radio that changed my life.

"It's my life / It's now or never / I ain't gonna live forever," sang Jon Bon Jovi. I got up and found a pen to use as a microphone. I turned the radio up and started belting out the words:

It's my life
It's now or never
I ain't gonna live forever
I just want to live while I'm alive
(It's my life)

It was then that I made up my mind to live more and work less.

Don't get me wrong: I was still a career-focused individual. I enjoyed the work I did. I wanted to continue making good money and climbing the corporate ladder. My change of heart was not about working; I just needed to put the *living* back in my life. It was time for me to remember how much I enjoyed being outdoors, cooking dinner, and enjoying a meal with my husband. I needed to enjoy a lazy Saturday morning without my smartphone or a Sunday afternoon without an anxiety attack. I craved balance, calmness, and harmony between what I did to earn a living and how I lived. I wanted to enjoy my work AND my life.

I was eager to remember who I was, what I valued in my life, and what I wanted to achieve—both professionally and personally. I yearned to rebalance my days, spending more time on the things I *wanted* to do and less time on things I felt I *had* to do. I needed to figure out how to set boundaries, say "no," work smarter, and do the important things—not everything.

During the following year, I did a lot of soul searching. I read books. I listened to my heart more than my head. I drew boundaries and took back my health and my relationships. I said "no" to things I didn't want to do, and spent my valuable time on the things I did want to do. I found my aliveness, happiness, and enjoyment of life.

And then I was promoted.

Of course I wasn't expecting it. I had spent a year enjoying my life. I had done the things at work that mattered most and left the rest for someone else. I had done all the things that I tell you about in this book, and what happened? I worked less, lived more, and wound up getting rewarded for it—both professionally and personally.

The world has changed a lot since I found my balance in 2002. Technology. Global business. Downsizing. Outsourcing. More collaboration and less hierarchy mean more people are needed to make a decision. Reduced budgets and increased scope mean we are all doing more work with fewer resources.

We—you and I—have also changed a lot since 2002. Growing children. Aging parents. Family demands. Expanding waistlines. Reduced energy. More responsibilities. Things move faster around us but our basic human desires haven't changed. We crave a life filled with our *wants*, not the *shoulds* and *should haves*. But how do we gain control of our lives? How do we deal with the external influences that tell us what we "should" be doing? How do we reprogram our addiction to perfection, overachievement, and constant performance? How do we stop the unstoppable from taking over?

"Work/life balance" is an overused phrase. When I hear people say, "I really want more work/life balance," I wonder if they truly want equal portions of work and life. Equal time spent at work, then at life, is simply impossible—at least if you want to have a life. What I believe they are really after is less quantity and more quality in all areas of their lives.

I would like you to consider, instead, the idea of living a life *in* balance. The difference between a life in balance and a work/life balance is that your approach comes from a place of understanding who you want to be now—not in the future, not in retirement, and not in a dream. The clarity that surrounds you when you are able to connect directly to your true sense of being feels like a weight lifting from your shoulders. You relax into knowing the answer to the question, "Why do you work so hard?" This grounding allows you to draw clearer lines between the important and the urgent, the want and the should, and *being more* instead of *doing more*. Living life in balance will mean working hard both professionally and personally, but with more harmony and clarity—and less stress.

Picture your daily life as a circle. Like a pie. Some days you have a bigger slice of career, some days you have a bigger slice of family, and some days you have a bigger slice just for you. In order to get to this point, however, you need to understand who you are (or who you want to be) in relation to those three pieces of pie and—even more important—have the fortitude to slice your pie the way *you* want and need, not accepting anyone else's cut.

Living a life in balance is not easy. For those of you whose own lives resemble my past, it's especially hard and requires a precarious balance between pragmatic actions and personal awareness. "To do" lists are just as important as dreams. Delegating is just as important as trusting. Ego management is about defining your worth by contribution, not title. Realistic has to befriend idealistic. Practical has to start dating theoretical. And sensible has to invite spiritual in for a visit. Perfect becomes good enough, overachieving takes a nap, and letting go becomes freedom. You'll feel a bit crazy. You'll feel a bit out of control. But you will be living in the moment.

This book will take you through the same journey I took myself—from too much tedious work and too little living to a life in balance. As any logically minded person would expect, we'll start by identifying why we are programmed the way we are and why that's gotten us where we are today. Yes, both the good and the ugly. Once we understand why we live the way we do, we'll spend some time thinking about the way we'd like to live. Maybe we are close, maybe we aren't—that's what we have to figure out and get comfortable with. After all, living a life in balance is only good if it's the life that you really want to be living.

Then we'll move on to the heart of the matter: How the heck do we efficiently and practically reduce the quantity—and increase the quality—of the work we do, thus creating time for fuller living? Once we have done some reprogramming, this will be much easier than you think. Trust me.

At the heart of our balancing success is our own physical and mental health. Without good mental and physical health, you cannot live a life in balance. Excellent mental and physical health allows you to live your life to its fullest capacity because it gives you energy, flexibility, confidence, and time.

I will not be talking to you about dieting or exercising in the context of looking better, but instead in the context of helping you to understand how the food you eat and the way you move your body creates the strength and clarity needed to find more balance in your life. It is easy to believe that taking time in your day for exercise or cooking a healthy meal could cause stress because you might lose the time needed to finish a project at work or take the kids to afterschool activities, but it's quite the opposite. You will find that eating well and being more physically active results in needing *less* time to finish the work project and having more time to enjoy the afterschool moments with your children.

By the time you hit the conclusion of this book, you will have found a destination you won't ever want to leave. Imagine finally waking up energized in the morning, excited about starting a new day, instead of waking up tired and stressed and worrying about all that needs to be done at work and at home. Fantasize about having the confidence to push back, dictate your schedule, and enjoy the work that you do while still being profoundly successful. Dream about what your life in balance really looks like, then use this book to make that dream a reality.

I almost titled this book "Live More, Work Less," but realized that simply working *less* is not the intention of my message, nor is it a realistic goal for many of us. This book is about *Living More* by understanding how to *Work Better*—in both your professional and personal lives. Working is an important factor in my life; besides paying my bills and buying the luxuries I enjoy, working professionally provides me the opportunity to use my brain, help others, and create change in the world. Working *personally* means contributing to my community, eating healthy food, exercising, and engaging in constant self-improvement. My work is an important part of my life, and I suspect the same is true for you. Inevitably, working better will mean that you *are* working less, because you will have clarified your focus, drawn your boundaries, and increased your productivity.

So, settle in and enjoy yourself. In the spirit of living more and working better, I have kept this book short enough to read on your next business trip (efficiency), included short activities that can be completed in real time (multitasking), and all of my health-oriented suggestions give you the biggest health bang for your time and money (productivity).

Here's to your life—after all, it's now or never.

Chapter 1

Why Do We Work So Hard?

There are many kinds of people in this world. Every day we encounter people who work as hard or harder than we do and we feel at home. Yet there are days when we meet someone who works half the hours we do and seems to have a fuller life than we do. How do they do that? Sure, there may be family money or some other financial windfall at work behind the scenes, but for the most part, it seems to be an attitude—a way of living or thinking—that they possess and we don't. So, if there are other work mentality options out there, how did we wind up in the league of overworkers?

The Work Hard Mentality Starts in Childhood

I was in second grade, Mrs. Morten's class, when I became aware of the rewards of achievement. Gold stars. Applause when you won a race. Invitations to become friends with other achievers. Popularity, acceptance, and safety were all waiting at the other end of achievement. Whether they had earned good grades or athletic success, the high achievers were the group to run with.

And so things progressed through elementary school. Entering sixth grade was a whole new world, with even more achievement hurdles. In addition to the honor roll, maintaining status in the popular crowd required better clothing, the right boyfriends, and more studying. But sixth grade proved to be a pivotal time in my life, as it held my first monumental failure.

My sixth grade year was spent in a middle school in Rye, New Hampshire. The basketball team was the highlight of every middle school boy's dream, while being on the cheerleading squad was the coveted prize for us girls. The cheerleading tryouts were brutal. The hours of after-school practice with fifty other hopeful girls created a competitive war zone. I had the voice, I had the splits, but darn it if I could nail my cartwheel.

Tryouts lasted two days. At the end of the second day, the list was taped to the gym wall, noting the girls who had successfully achieved goddess status and were admitted to the cheerleading squad. We ran to the piece of legal-sized paper on the wall like we were racing for an Olympic gold medal. Pushing and shoving, squealing and crying, it was finally my turn to get a glance at the list. Gayle Ware. Gayle Ware. Come on. Come on. Where was my name?

My name was nowhere on that list. I was devastated. This was the end of a dream of a life filled with friends, happiness, and high society. I was going to be relegated to a life of unpopularity, nonacceptance, and ridicule. I had failed.

While my crushed sixth-grade cheerleading dream might seem trivial, I have come to see that it was that specific situation that created my path to overachievement through the better part of my teenage years. By not making the cheerleading squad, I let my friends down, I let my parents down, and I proved to the whole world that I was a failure. At least, that was how I felt. That day I decided I would never feel those feelings again. I would succeed in everything I put my efforts into going forward—for my parents, my friends, and the whole world.

Growing up, we all receive messages every day from our surroundings. At home, they range from the form of basic childhood discipline (make your bed, clean your room, eat everything on your plate) to more evolved messaging about how life is lived (work hard, earn money, be a good person). Slowly, we begin to put things together in our minds. *If I make my bed, clean my room, and eat everything on my plate, I am "good." If I don't make my bed, clean my room, and eat everything on my plate, I am "bad."* If I work hard, I win. If I don't work hard, I fail. These messages gradually become relevant for academic achievements, sports achievements, musical achievements, and work achievements. For me, rewards were recognition, accolades, popularity, and the comfort of knowing that I hadn't let anyone down.

As children, our psyches are in a delicate state. Learned behaviors develop as a way to protect ourselves. In my case, I learned that the harder I worked, the more rewarded I became. The higher my grades, the more teachers praised my work. The better my flute playing, the more solos I received. The better I was at everything I did, the more I pleased those around me; the more pleased people were, the happier I was.

Until I hit the point of diminishing happiness returns.

It was my senior year of college and I was exhausted. I knew I had to perform academically to secure a good job after graduation. My roommate of four years was emotionally bullying me into being her "best friend." I was working during my free hours to earn money to pay for my room and board. Most of my friends and family believed that my romantic relationship was emotionally unhealthy and that severing the relationship would be good for me. I felt like my life was all about everyone else and I felt guilty that I felt bad about that. I was tired of being what everyone else expected of me, yet I was scared to let anyone down. I needed someone neutral to talk to.

There was a group of graduate students who had set up free therapy services for undergraduate students. I was scared to make an appointment, but I needed an outlet and there was no better choice. I walked into the counselor's office and the first thing I said was, "I'm sure you have better things to do with your time than talk to me about how sick and tired I am of trying to be great." After that, we met every week for an hour.

We focused on two words during most of our time together:

Perfectionism: The refusal to accept any standard short of perfection (perfection being the action or process of improving something until it is faultless or as faultless as possible).

Overachiever: One who is excessively dedicated to achieving success.

What The Matrix *Teaches Us About Society's Influence*

The Matrix was a 1999 movie staring Keanu Reeves and Laurence Fishburne. It was a groundbreaking moving for its visual and sound effects, and it won Academy Awards in both categories.

The story, however, was hotly debated. Some criticized it as being reminiscent of old school sci-fi works, while others found it intriguing. Personally, I think they all missed the point.

Neo (Reeves), the main character, is a computer hacker wooed from his job by Morpheus (Fishburne) to live his life outside the "matrix," free from the "mind prison" created by computers.

The matrix in the movie is analogous to society in our everyday lives. In the movie, the matrix exists all around us. We exist *within* the matrix. In the same way, our society defines what is acceptable, what is normal, what is good, and what is bad. We are taught that to succeed in life, we must look, act, and have what is acceptable, normal, and good.

A trim body, a big house, an expensive car, a good-looking family, a job with a title—these have all become icons of "the good life." So we work hard to achieve them and perceive anything short of having them as failure. We enjoy pushing ourselves to the attainment of these goals. We are goal-oriented, type-A high-achievers who love being pushed to higher and higher performance.

But here's where things get interesting. Once Neo is successfully outside the matrix, he sees things as they are, not as he's been taught to believe. His mind is released from prison and he begins to think differently. Thinking differently is not easy and takes practice, but slowly Neo starts to understand how to use his mind to create his own reality. He sees himself clearly for the first time. He realizes that the accepted rules of society don't always need to be accepted as truth or reality.

The scene in the movie that best depicts this concept takes place when Neo is waiting to meet the Oracle (long story, but you don't need the background to understand the point). While waiting, Neo meets a young boy who is also waiting to meet the Oracle. The boy is holding a spoon, which he proceeds to bend with nothing but his mind. Their conversation goes like this:

Boy: (to Neo): Do not try to bend the spoon. That's impossible. Instead, only try to realize the truth.

Neo: What truth?

Boy: There is no spoon.

Neo: (because there obviously *is* a spoon): There is no spoon?

Boy: Then you'll see that it is not the spoon that bends, it is only yourself.

I didn't understand it the first time, nor probably the second or third time I watched the movie. It was only when I started to question my conformation to society's definition of right, acceptable, and successful that the boy's comment to Neo became clear.

The spoon is what society puts forward to us as right, wrong, acceptable, successful, good, bad, etc. We see it in all forms of media, we hear it from parents/teachers/friends, and we eat it, sleep it, and work it. We call it reality.

5

What *The Matrix* teaches us is that, in fact, we are the ones in control of creating our own reality. It is for us to define what is good or bad, what makes us happy or sad. The beauty of our situation, versus Neo's, is that we don't have to take a pill or live in a really decrepit space machine to live outside of the matrix. We each have the power to define our own version of success.

But, because the "matrix" is all around us, living our lives on our terms—independent of caring what others think to be right or wrong—is not easy. It took Neo a full movie before he was able to see through the matrix. It will take us longer, but it all starts with understanding that you create the reality of your daily life. The sooner you can see through what society has defined as your reality, the sooner you can free your mind, take control of your own existence, exit the matrix, and move into your life.

> *The sooner you see past what society has defined as reality, the sooner you can live freely, take control of your own existence, and move into your life.*

The Worst Offender: Corporate Culture

Childhood leaves us with some deep-rooted thoughts and behaviors. Society fuels our need for conformity and defines acceptable boundaries.

Corporate culture reinforces the best and the worst of both of these things.

Are you a type-A personality, wealth crusader, and ambition junky with a strong mental and physical drive for success, a deep-rooted need to prove yourself worthy, a do-what-it-takes mentality, and an unhealthy respect for hierarchy? The corporate world has a job for you! In return for all of your overachiever traits, the corporate world will offer you challenge, negative reinforcement, money, titles, and hundreds of other people just like you who will provide competition and mess with your confidence. It's a match made in perfectionist heaven.

I am that person. I took that corporate challenge. I became a full-fledged workaholic. I worked hard so that I could live well, yet was working so much, I never had the opportunity to enjoy how well I was supposed to be living. The irony of that reality wasn't lost on me.

In today's world, we have the additional pressures of stock prices, sales targets, budget cuts, and job security. Make one bad step and *whammo*—you could be out of a job because you cost too much, you weren't checking your email at exactly the right time, or someone else in a lower-cost location (or even some piece of technology) could be doing your job at half the cost. These pressures are corporate enablers to all of us who are up for challenge, determined to succeed, in a constant search of perfection, and would be embarrassed by failure. The more demanding our professional environment becomes, the harder we work to prove our worth.

While corporations offer programs and opportunities to work smarter, focus on what is important, take risks, and contribute to a job you enjoy, corporate *culture* frequently positively reinforces harder workers who react to urgency, are scared to take risks, and continue in jobs they don't enjoy because they need to make a living and don't want to piss anyone off.

Corporate culture supports our childhood needs to be accepted, approved of, safe—and successful.

Perfectionist, Performance Addict, Overachiever— What We Have Become

So, where does it all leave us? We are left feeling that we need to do everything, and do it all right. We constantly demand more and more from ourselves, equating "busyness" with worthiness. We strive over and over again for more and more. In short, we have become a gang of perfectionists, performance addicts, and overachievers.

Don't get me wrong. Perfectionists, performance addicts, and overachievers are very successful people. Most of the time, they truly enjoy the challenging work and rewards earned from their success. But there almost always comes a tipping point—a point where the rewards received don't measure up to the effort and time expended. Resentment, exhaustion, and bitterness replace challenge, excitement, and the need for material rewards.

You and I have hit this tipping point. It is time to thank our childhood messaging for helping us grow, and to recognize that we are now adults and no longer need that safety. It is time to define for ourselves who we really want to be in this world, regardless of society's definitions. It is time to decide that our hard work should be directed to doing what we love most and feel contributes most completely to our world.

What we have become can now be our springboard for where we need to go.

Chapter 2

You Can Alter Your Reality

Just because we are built a certain way does not mean we can't change. Just because we have inherited and developed certain traits doesn't mean we can't change. Just because we have believed certain old truths doesn't mean we can't believe in new truths.

We decide to rear our children differently than our parents did because there were things about our childhoods that we'd prefer not to duplicate. We change our minds about what we are wearing, where we want to eat, and what to watch on television every day without thinking twice. We used to believe in Santa Claus, but now we don't. We alter our reality every day without batting an eyelash. So how can we alter our work/life relationship to truly start living the life in our lives?

> *How can we truly start living the life in our lives?*

Who Am I?

If you want to alter your current reality, you must start by understanding where you are, then identify where you want to go.

Have you ever taken a few hours out of your day to truly ponder the question of who you are? You can start with the obvious: I am a wife, husband, partner, mother, father, sister, brother, aunt, uncle, daughter, son, career professional, runner, volunteer … . The list can go on and on. Your cultural background, hobbies, interests, physical abilities, and place in your family all describe you, as well. But is your outward-facing you the same as the inner you?

Carving time out of your current life schedule to search for the more inward answer to the question "Who am I?" is worth the effort. Taking a few hours to quiet your mind and think about who you really are will allow you to free yourself from who you think you are—or who you think you *should* be. When you take this time, you can identify what defines you as a real person inside, not just from the outside.

As you can imagine, the first time I tried this exercise, I felt a bit uncomfortable. It was similar to my feelings in yoga class when the class was asked to let our minds be clear and free from all that we were thinking. I felt irritated that I was being forced to give up control of my mind to a woman who smelled like incense. I was sure that freeing her mind was easy for her to do—I bet her life was nowhere near as full as mine, nor her responsibilities as important as mine. I was sure that if I spent my days teaching yoga, my mind would be clear as a bell. I started to get annoyed at the sound of her voice, which of course only served to agitate my mind—a far cry from keeping it clear and calm.

I didn't give up, though. I was challenged to clear my mind, so yes, I would meet that challenge. I was also a little curious about what it would feel like to have a clear mind, which was free of "to do" lists, calendar events, and shopping lists. But it didn't happen during a yoga class. In fact, it happened at mile five of a ten-mile training run.

I was training for a marathon that year. I don't actually enjoy the physical effort of running, but I had chosen to run because running is a form of exercise that is easy to take with you anywhere you go, doesn't require a lot of equipment, is an individual activity, and doesn't include people staring and you. Plus, I love being outdoors. I decided to run a marathon because I felt the need to accomplish something, so I set my sights on 26.2 miles of hell.

During the first three miles of every training run, my mind was filled with thoughts of how hot it was, how my knees hurt, and how my breathing sounded like the last gasp for air before death. It usually wasn't until mile four that I was able to relax into my run. I realized early in my training program that since I would be training for the next six months to be able to run 26.2 miles, I might as well just relax, settle in, and enjoy the experience. On one particular day, I was scheduled to run ten miles. Based on my average speed, ten miles would usually take me about two hours. So I settled into the fact that, on that beautiful Sunday morning—when what I really wanted was to be sleeping in with my husband—I would instead spend two hours running. One foot in front of the other for two hours.

The sun was warm without being hot. The trail had a few other people crazy enough to be up early on a Sunday morning running, but early morning runners are always nice. We wave and nod as we huff and puff past each other. I was running through some woods, which have always been a source of peace and comfort for me. All of a sudden, I hit mile five (my turnaround point) and realized that the last time I had had a coherent thought in my head was when I felt my knee buckle at mile two. I had just run three miles with a completely clear mind.

There are many different schools of thought on meditating, several of which support the idea that you can meditate while walking or running. Regardless of how you come to it, the end game of all meditation is to clear your mind—how you attain that status is up to you. The irony of the fact that clearing my mind in yoga class was irritating and difficult, yet I could become crystal clear while on a ten-mile training run, was not lost on me—a woman addicted to her performance.

I was forty years old that year. I wasn't one to shy away from a fortieth birthday. In fact, to this day, I celebrate every year I get older. If we are lucky, every year that goes by is another year closer to feeling completely comfortable in our skin, understanding who we really are, and caring less about what other people think. My fortieth year of life was when I started my journey to understand more about who I really wanted to be in my lifetime and ended my dependence on what other people might think about my discoveries. (That year was also the year I realized that I did not look good in leggings and found the much more flattering yoga pant!)

I had been with the same company for nineteen years and had reached a level of seniority at which I spent more time on corporate bureaucracy and profit management than on truly helping people grow. I was torn. The higher up I went, the more my job would require travel, mandatory socialization, and becoming a "talking head" for corporate priorities. I decided that it was time to explore more about me, to look deep inside and really define who I was, what I believed in, what made me happy, and what drove me to action. I wasn't unhappy, I just knew I could be happier. And, at forty years old, it was a perfect time to make changes.

My next training run was twelve miles. Looking forward to my newfound mile-five clarity, I decided to use it to my advantage. I found a package of Post-it notes (the world's greatest invention, in my mind) and a pen, stuffed them in the pocket of my running shirt, and went. My goal was to spend time contemplating the question "Who am I?" The first three miles were spent as they always were, in agony. Mile four, I started to relax. Mile five, I was in a zone. Mile six, I asked myself, "Who am I?" and let the thoughts run wild.

I am an introvert by nature.

I am a lover of nature.

I am a world traveler.

I have an overwhelming desire to be in control of my own fate.

I am a woman who cares deeply about her family.

I am married to my soul mate and nothing is more important to me than being with him.

I am honest. Really, really honest. (Sometimes, too honest—it's been known to get me in trouble.)

I am a helper, supporter, and developer of other people.

I am okay with never being a supermodel.

I am well-off financially, more than I ever imagined possible.

I am healthy—physically and mentally.

Each time I had a thought, I wrote it on a Post-it note. When I got home from my run, I transferred all the sticky pads to a notebook (the second greatest invention). I then closed the notebook, took a shower, and enjoyed the rest of my day. I felt light, carefree, and unburdened that day.

Let's stop here for a moment. Find a writing utensil. If you are e-reading this book, you will also need a piece of paper. If you are reading the paperback version of this book, I've included pages in the Appendix of the book to make exercises like this easier for you. Flip to the page titled "**WHO AM I?**" Doing these exercises in real time will save you time (you will not have to come back and do this exercise another time), and create the most impact (you are in the mood, in the flow, in the moment, so take advantage of your energies and make them work for you). Now write down whatever pops into your mind when I ask you the question: "Who are you?" You can use some of my answers above as a guide. Do not judge, feel bad, or otherwise chastise yourself for anything you write down. Just get it all out on paper; then put it away and continue reading. (I'll wait.)

A few days after my "writing run," I decided I would end work promptly at 5:00 p.m. I got home, poured myself a glass of wine, got comfortable on the couch, and decided to take a few minutes before starting dinner to look at my notebook, which I had left closed on my desk ever since my run. When I saw what I had written, I felt all of the stress of the workday melt away. Then I recounted my day, and felt my stress level rise once again. My day had been spent approving policies, playing the extrovert in meetings to prove that I had something to say, saying "yes" to decisions and activities that I wasn't fully vested in, and figuring out ways to cut costs to ensure funding for executive bonuses (including my own).

I spent most of my days being someone who wasn't me.

In essence, I had spent most of my day being someone other than who I thought I was—someone almost exactly the opposite of who I was when I was running. I wasn't sad and I wasn't resentful. I was just very interested in the observation of how my answers to "Who am I?" aligned, or didn't, with my current reality. How about that? Sometimes, just taking a few quiet minutes of observation is much more productive than action or judgment. It's hard, but much more productive. I encourage you to do this same reflection exercise a week from now, using the Who I Am? list you just created (and try not to peek at it in the meantime).

While the work I did on getting more in tune with my inner me was great, that doesn't mean I didn't also enjoy elements of my outer self. While there were parts of my job/life that were contradictory to the inner me, there were also many things that were in alignment. My love of travel and my good health were supported by the influence and monetary rewards that came with my seniority. As a human Resources director, I had made a career out of helping, supporting, and developing other people. My seniority and rank allowed for enough autonomy and flexibility that I had a level of control over my work product and schedule.

So the question became: "Who do I want to be?"

When you ask yourself who you want to be — and give yourself honest answers — your outward reality and inner truths synthesize to define your desired reality.

Who Do You Want To Be? You already have a good start on answering that question from the work we did answering Who Am I? because, usually, we find that who we are deep inside is our desired state of being. We just have to figure out how to best unveil our inner selves in our outward realities.

Now is the perfect time for another quick break. Again, writing utensil and piece of paper needed (flip to the end of the book for quick, easy access to a blank piece of paper titled **"WHO DO I WANT TO BE?"**). Take a moment to reflect, then start writing your responses to the question "Who Do You Want To Be?" Don't hesitate. Don't think too hard. Just reflect, write, reflect, and write. When you're finished, just put the paper away (or flip back to this spot) and continue onward.

Based on what I had written down, I found that I had a pretty good idea of who I wanted to be:

> I wanted to connect my inner desire to help and support people with my outward professional success so that I could help and support even more people.

> I wanted to bind my love of anything healthy and natural with my influence and leadership position to benefit others' overall quality of life.

> I wanted to speak when I truly had something of quality to contribute and let those words create my credibility.

> I wanted to travel with my husband, not my colleagues.

> I wanted to love my family and set an example for my nieces and nephews by living my individuality to its fullest.

Again, this took some time to understand. Masterpieces are not created in one working session. Once a week I would schedule a date with myself, usually an hour, and *always* with a glass of wine. I set this time aside to review what I had accomplished that week. This was to remind myself that I had gotten a lot done and that it was okay to take a few hours to reenergize. Then, I would take some time to review my Who Am I? list and my Who Do I Want To Be? list. I would account for how many times during the past week I was able to make the connection between Who I Am and Who I Want To Be.

It might have been small things, like cooking and eating dinner with my husband without email interruption, or an early morning run in the woods. It may have been big items, like holding my team responsible for setting and meeting health objectives as part of their performance rating or delegating policy development so that I could focus on leadership development.

Your turn. Using your Who Am I and Who Do I Want to Be lists as guides, try living in the next week in congruency with your lists. At the end of the week, pull out your Who Am I? list and your Who Do I Want to Be? list. Review your past week in relation to both of these lists. How did you do? Remember, you are new to this, and you might not have done as well as you hoped. But, whether big or small, the point is to reflect on who you are and make the connection to who you want to be on a regular basis. You have to keep these two ideals at the forefront of your daily life.

The more we do this, the closer we come to living in congruency.

Your Perception Is Your Reality

The world is full of media sources that talk about the basic idea of changing your mind to change your life. The market is flooded with books filled with positive daily affirmations that exist for the sole purpose of challenging you to think differently (more *positively*, of course) about you and your life. At the same time, meditation, in its various forms, is also about training the mind to hold a more positive outlook.

But to truly change your mind, to look at the world through a different lens, to think differently about yourself, people, or circumstances in your life is not an easy task. For most of us, our mind is cluttered with the everyday realities of what needs to get done. Deadlines at work, a child's dance lessons, grocery lists, home repair projects, extra curricular activities—our minds wake us up in the morning and make it difficult to go to sleep at night. They are chattering away at us constantly. Our minds not only keep track of everything that needs to be done, they also silently comment on us and the world around us. We constantly hear the voice in our heads critiquing how we look, what we say, what others say to us, how others looked at us, what we should have done, what we didn't do—it's a never-ending script running through our heads.

> ### *Our minds create our realities.*

Along with channeling our perceptions, our minds are also the sole creators of our realities. When your mind is made up to do something, you do it. When your mind tells you how to dress, speak, act, and live "appropriately," you take the "appropriate" actions. Our minds filter information from the external world and serve it to us in a way we understand, based on our values and beliefs. It is exactly this skill, this ability to create our reality, that makes our minds so powerful.

Review your Who I Am and Who Do I Want to Be lists. How many times, either while creating those lists or in review of them, did your mind tell you something different than what you read? For example, I am an introvert by nature. When I first wrote that on my list, my mind told me that being an introvert meant that I was shy, and if I'm shy, then I won't be as successful as I want to be because I need to be outgoing, or extroverted, to successfully climb the corporate ladder. Where on earth did I get that idea? From the media, from books, and from people who have said over the years that I need to be seen and heard to be successful. My mind has captured those messages and feeds them back to me when I decide to feel something seemingly in opposition with what is acceptable. So over time I have learned that if I am an introvert, I will fail.

Wait a minute! Being an introvert is so much more complex than just not being the first one to state an opinion. As a matter of fact, there are now studies that show that introverts make great leaders because they are thoughtful, calming, know the benefit of alone time, and usually think before they speak—all of which are great qualities leading to personal and professional success. What Do I Want to Be? I want to be someone who is known, personally and professionally, as a thought leader—and I'd like for that reputation to afford the lifestyle I desire. Right here, I'm going to change my response to the fact that I'm an introvert. I'm going to celebrate the fact that being an introvert may be the one thing that leads to my overall success. I've changed my mind. Being an introvert is not failure, it's success.

While changing our minds is not easy work, we *all* have the power to choose a different response and change the course of our futures.

> *Changing your mind is not easy work, but it gives you the power to change the course of your future.*

My perception of life used to be that the only way to make a good living was to work as hard as you possibly can until you retire; then (in retirement), you will be able to do what you really love. John Bon Jovi helped me see things differently. My perception of life today is that everyone can make a living doing what they love, they just have to take action. I have created that reality for myself by leaving my corporate job three years ago to build my own Executive Health and Leadership Coaching company. I work with corporate executives around the world on the concept of changing their minds. Here is one of my favorite client exercises.

This exercise is called "living in a fantasy world." Everyone has a fantasy world. This is the alternate universe we retire to when things get really hard in the real world. Each fantasy world usually includes the perfect job (if a job at all), all the wealth you desire, all the time you desire to spend on your biggest interests, and usually a slightly-better-looking version of yourself, and your family.

Let's start small and envision a "fantasy day." Again, flip to the end of the book and find the blank page to capture your fantasy day (titled **"FANTASY DAY"**), or use a blank piece of paper near you. Now, think about what your perfect day would look like. When would you get up in the morning? What would you eat for breakfast? What type of work (if any) would you be accomplishing? Get a clear picture in your mind of what life would look like in your alternate reality.

Then, before you read any further, take a good look at what you've written. You've created, on that page, your perfect fantasy day—the start of your journey to your fantasy world. Now I want you to write down the answer to this question: Why can't you do that? Don't overthink it. Don't think up excuses. Allow yourself to rationally consider your fantasy day and truly consider why you can't have that perfect day.

I know it's not easy to move from your current reality to dwelling in your alternate universe 24/7, but that's not the intention of the exercise. The intention of the exercise is to answer the questions "Why?" and "Why can't you?" Sometimes there are very real barriers, but most of the time people get a bit frustrated because they cannot think of a genuine reason why they can't live their fantasy lives. They perceive that they can't for a variety of reasons, and usually their minds are simply made up that it's impossible, but when they have to answer the question, "Why can't you?" they realize there actually could be a different way of thinking.

This trick works well with an even narrower application. For example, let's say that you are working too much and really want to reduce your work time by one hour every day. So, in your fantasy world, you imagine working one less hour each day. Once you have that in mind, ask yourself: "Why can't I just close my computer and stop working one hour earlier every day?"

Your answer may look something like: "Because I have too many emails to respond to." The perception here is that you have to respond to all of your emails because that's what is expected of you. I ask you, though, are all of your emails related to work you need to complete by tomorrow morning? I would guess that, if you are honest, the answer would be "No. In fact most of them are informational—or from groups of people hitting the 'reply to all' button."

So, why can't you close your computer and stop working one hour earlier every day? My clients usually come up with a few more reasons that are just as dissectible as the email excuse before we finally get to the real reason they are unable to close their computers and stop working: They are scared, worried, or think they are much more important than they really are. Once we get to that realization, we can talk about those feelings.

Assume that we have gone through these steps and you are beginning to realize that you can turn off your computer an hour earlier every day. You have changed your mind. The new perception that maybe, just maybe, you are not needed on email has now become your working reality. You are now on your way to changing your life by ending your work day one hour earlier.

If you are able to apply this concept to something as small as shutting down from work one hour earlier each day, imagine what more you could accomplish if you changed your mind about your job responsibilities, what you do in your personal time, where you live, or anything in your life.

Challenge your perceptions. Ask yourself "Why?" Think about your responses. Change your mind, and you will change your life.

> *Change your mind. Change your life.*

Walk Your New Reality with Confidence

The hardest part about living the life you've dreamed of is doing it with confidence. Your mind will continue to remind you that things get done a certain way—the way you and those around you have always done them—and that, when you question those paradigms, you are doing something bad. Society will continue to display the world around you as it "should" be.

You might feel uncomfortable, different from people around you, or just plain wrong. Or, you might feel relieved, invigorated, refreshed, and energized. You are bucking the system, after all—you are breaking out of your constant normality. But the more confidently you walk in your new reality, the more you will change your own mind and the minds of those around you. The more you impact the people around you, the more your new reality will become a norm. It's a never-ending circle of confidence and success.

The year after I wasn't promoted, the perception that I had held for so long (that hard work always reaped rewards) was an easy one to change. Obviously, I had worked hard and had not been rewarded. So I created my new reality—one in which I would finally put myself and the life I wanted to live at the top of my priority list. The first thing I wanted to do was start my workday at 8:00 a.m. so I could get an hour of exercise in the morning without having to get up any earlier. (Prior to this, I would start my workday at 7:00 a.m. to ensure that I was at my desk and already fully caught up on email and voicemail so my productive workday could start at 8:00 a.m.)

The first two weeks of a new routine are always the most difficult, but if you can make it through those, you have a great chance for success. When I changed my mind, I got up, exercised, and started working at 8:00 a.m. Even though I felt guilty and constantly wondered who might be looking for me with some urgent project, disappointed when they didn't see me at my desk, I continued with my routine. I wanted this new reality, so I determined that I was going to work to make it happen.

On Thursday of that first week, my supervisor asked me if I was feeling okay. I knew very well why she was asking; in her mind, I had been late for work the past few days and, thus, it must have been related to my health. I was afraid to tell her the truth. I felt a rush of apprehension pass through my body; I had been found out, my boss was disappointed, I had failed, I could never tell her the truth. Then I stopped, took a deep breath, and remembered how excited I was about my new reality. That excitement gave me the confidence to truthfully answer her question. I told her that I was fine and, in fact, I had never felt better. She didn't have to know anything more.

Part of the art of walking your new reality with confidence is not prematurely reacting to someone else's perceived disappointment in you and your decisions. Because I was so sure the conversation wasn't over, I didn't immediately defend myself. Instead, I simply waited for my supervisor to ask me more questions.

There were no further questions that day but, on Friday afternoon, my supervisor stopped me before I left for the weekend and asked if she should assume that I would be making a habit of coming in at 8:00 a.m. every day.

Again, my initial reflex was to assume she was put out with me because I was not living up to her expectations and that I should probably give up my new routine to save my job. Dramatic, yes, but we all know this is what goes through our minds when we change something about ourselves. We look for confirmation from others that we did the right thing but expect that we have disappointed them. Conversely, if we weren't expecting to disappoint, why would we look for confirmation in the first place?

After a deep breath, I told her that, yes, 8:00 a.m. was my new normal. I then went on to explain that I had prioritized getting back into shape, and to do so, I was exercising before coming to work every morning. I explained that not only had I felt better all week, but that I was also pleased that I hadn't let any important work slip and had found that I was more alert, productive, and creative during working hours. Then, because I respected her and my job, I said I hoped she had seen the same from my performance in the past week. I did not apologize for my actions, but I inquired about *her perception* of the situation. Just as we can question our own perceptions to help alter our personal reality, so can we help others do the same by questioning their perceptions.

She laughed and confirmed that she was more than pleased with my performance. She also said that she was relieved, as she had worried that my new work normal was due to something bad that had happened in my life. We ended the day talking about our individual workout routines and how they helped with stress management.

While I was changing my mental reality, I also successfully lost five pounds that month—while never missing a step at work.

Confidence is a difficult trait to develop. Some people are born outwardly confident, but, as we all know, many of the most confident people have developed their confident exteriors as a way to hide very insecure interiors. The type of confidence I'm referring to, however, is sometimes easier to develop than what is required to seem confident speaking or performing in front of others or carrying your head high when you don't like the way you look. Those are *external* confidences.

The type of confidence I'm asking you to develop is the *internal* confidence in yourself that says that you can change your habits, your mind, and your life. The confidence that you can do things differently because you *are* different and you don't have to be like everyone else to be successful. The confidence that you only get one life to lead, so you better find a way to do it the way you want to do it before you waste it. The kind of confidence that, when challenged by others to conform, will make you laugh because you know a secret to living a better life that they never will.

> *Confidence gives you the power be yourself, and vice versa.*

Have confidence in your power to truly be you. Trust that the real you will still be loved, will still make a living, and will make a bigger difference in the lives of others. And, once you've got that confidence, don't allow all of your dream-life visioning to be subject to other people's evaluations of whether you are right or not. Stand up for what you want and what you believe in. Have the confidence to know that what you think is right for you really is right for you. Be pleasantly surprised when others react positively, and feel sorry for those who react negatively.

Because when you harness your power and see the world through a new lens of confidence, you have successfully altered your reality.

> *When you harness your power to see the world with confidence, you will successfully alter your reality.*

Chapter 3

The Realist's Guide to Less Work and More Life

I'm a practical gal. I have my feet firmly planted on the ground. I existed in the corporate world for twenty-five years and fully appreciate the pace and demands of a high-powered position. I am known for thinking straight, talking straight, and getting things done. I am pragmatic. I have no time for airy-fairy, woo-woo, or nice-to-haves. I believe that only feasible, easy to implement, and workable ideas will elicit action from you all, so that's what I'm giving you here. Sure, you and I did a bit of soul searching in the previous chapters, but now it's down to business. It's time to use your type-A personality, action-oriented approach and your "no time for nonsense" traits to your advantage. It's time to work overtime on reducing your workload.

> *It's time for us to work on your workload.*

The "Want To Do" List vs. the "Have To Do" List

It is the bane of our existence. *It* is the meaning of our days. *It* is the measure of our abilities. *It* is our excuse to work more. *It* is social talk at a cocktail party and bragging rights at a meeting. *It* is the backbone of our everyday living.

It is our "to do" list.

Whether personal or professional—and most likely both— our "to do" lists are the dictators of our days.

Having a list of everything you need to get done is a good thing. As I grow older and my memory isn't what it used to be, I especially appreciate having that list by my side to provide me with a constant state of comfort and sanity. I know what I need to do every day, every week, and every year to hit my goals, get paid, enjoy my vacation time, stay healthy, maintain friendships, and contribute to my family.

We've all been taught, whether in time management classes or through reading stress management articles, that the best remedy for this "too much to do and not enough time" illness is to stop and write down exactly what we need to do.

So, in the morning, you take pen in hand and, as your mind thinks, your hand writes. Or, more likely, as your mind thinks, your fingers type. However you manage the process of getting what's in your head into some sort of list is unimportant. The act of clearing your head is what you're trying to do.

You take a slight breath of relief as you are finally able to stop thinking about what needs to be done and can easily look at a list of items that need to be completed by the end of the day. *Phew.* Crisis almost averted. Now, a quick meeting with your calendar over your morning cup of coffee and you are able to integrate what needs to be done with when you are able to get it done.

Inevitably, there is too much to do and not enough time, but somehow we feel a sense of empowerment and control over our lives when we are able to visualize the hours in our day that we will use to get things done. Sitting at our desks with our cups of coffee, able to view everything that needs to get done, makes us feel important. After all, look at all the things that need to get done—with a list like that, we must be important.

But almost better than the "to do" list itself is the feeling of accomplishment as you cross items off the list. You start the day with twenty items on your list. You've got a full day ahead of you. Reports to finish, clients to meet, proposals to

review, research to do, kids to take to school, food to prepare, bills to pay—they're all part of the busy professional's
day. No problem.

At the end of that busy day, you take a look at your list.
Whether you used checkmarks, drew lines through your items,
or claimed triumph with a big red X, taking inventory of all
the things you have done that day will make you feel good all
over. You came, you saw, and you conquered.

Many times, at the end of an exceptionally long day, I will
get more of a feeling of triumph from crossing items off of
my "to do" list than I felt completing the items themselves.

We enjoy organizing and controlling our time with our lists.
We crave that euphoric sense of accomplishment when we
cross items off our lists, one at a time, purposefully, with a
feeling of empowerment. So the process continues, day in and
day out, and our lives move forward; until that inevitable day
when we add more to our lists than we are able to check off.

The professionals I work with list their never-ending "to
do" lists as one of their primary sources of stress. For most
people, the point in time where the number of items to be
done supersedes the number of items you can confidently
draw a red line through is the tipping point of stress. Gone
is the feeling of control as you add items and the sense
of accomplishment as you mark them completed. Instead,
control and accomplishment are replaced by a feeling of being overwhelmed and defeated. It is at this point that most
people make a tragic decision—they decide that the only
way to survive is to spend more hours working to reduce
their "to do" lists.

What if I were to tell you that there is a way to reduce the
number of items you need to do every day? What if I could
provide you with ultimate control over what you have to get
done every day? Would you think I was crazy? Would you
read on to amuse yourself simply because you know it could
happen for others, but never for you? Would you decide that it

is worth reading further, on the off chance that I can offer you something that would mean less time spent working every day?

Here is what you need to know:

You can have ultimate control over your "to do" list by making it a list of things you *want* to do, not everything you feel you *have* to do. Focus on *what* you are putting on the list, not *how much* is on your list. After all, you don't have to do everything.

At first read, I'm sure that sounds obvious. But I encourage you to read that paragraph again, over and over, until you truly understand the essence of its message.

The "to do" list is another subtle message of being worthy and deserving handed to us by our childhood, society, and the corporate environment. In this case, size does matter. The longer our list is, the more important we feel we are because we feel we have a lot of people relying on us to do a lot of things. The more items we add to our list, the more we feel we are needed. The more items we can add *and* delete from our list, the more deserving we feel we are of our compensation, our time off, or any other perks we might receive for a job well done.

Let's step away from our historical programming and focus on the new reality we defined in Chapter Two.

Wouldn't it feel wonderful to spend more time every day doing what we want to do and less time doing what we don't want to do? You could feel uncomfortable at first, as you experience feelings of slacking off, unresponsiveness, and even boredom due to dropping items off your list. But, as quickly as you drop your unimportant items off the list, you will have time for more important items. Whether those items are professionally attached or personally focused, they are where you want your attention to be focused. These are not other people's priorities, they are your own, and a "to do" list focused on *your* priorities is a mighty wonderful way to confidently walk in your new reality.

While talking about turning our shoulds into wants is inspiring, let's think practically for a moment. We have a list of items that need to be done and regardless of how we feel about them, we won't get rewarded until they are completed. OK—time to tackle that "to do" list.

Once again, you will find pages at the end of this book reserved for these exercises. After all, I want you to be able to get the most out of these recommendations so you don't add additional actions to your "to do" list, like "Go back and do exercises in Gayle's book." Do them now, while they are fresh and you are in the mood. If you have your own source of paper, by all means, use what's comfortable for you. Otherwise, use the page in the Appendix titled "**MY WHYS AND MY WHATS**". Doing the exercise is what's important, not the medium.

1) **Discover Your Whys and Your Whats**. Reread the lists you created during the "Who Am I?" and "Who Do I Want to Be?" exercises you did in Chapter Two as a way to reengage in the life reality you want to create. Now, ask yourself: "What are my Whys?" (Why do you work? Why do you volunteer? Why did you have children? Why are you here?) Another question that will help generate good answers is "What are my Whats?" (What do you want to be? What do you want to leave as a legacy? What do you want people to say about you? What do you enjoy most in life? What do you want to fill your days doing?) As with all of these exercises, just write things down that pop into your mind. Don't judge your answers, don't overthink them, just react to what you feel in your gut.

2) **Create Categories**. Reread your Whys and Whats. Find the centering themes. Family, friends, work, volunteering; whatever stuff seems to draw most of your attention. Now, take the themes you see in your answers and create four categories. Why four? Because

if there are too many categories, your list will be too long. Too few categories, and you will be combining too many important elements of your life. Yes, three categories could work, as could five, but be cognizant of your tendencies to simplify or overcommit. (Plus, it's easy to divide a piece of paper into four.) My four categories are: Career, Marriage, Extended Family/Friends, and Personal Health. These four things are the most important things in my life. They represent who I want to be, how I want to live, and what I want to leave in this world. These four categories hold the things I want to spend quality time on every week to ensure that they flourish and thrive. These are my anchors, my big rocks, my categories. Write yours down on your WHYS and WHATS page so you don't forget them.

3) **Start Your "To Do" List**. Turn to the next page at the end of the book titled "**WANT TO DO**" list. You'll see that I have sectioned this page into four quadrants. Each quadrant will be titled with one of your four categories. So, go ahead, and fill those titles in now. You may be feeling that the categories are a bit broad to accommodate a detailed "to do" list on one piece of paper. If so, you've got great instincts—because you're right. The categories are meant to be broad because they are your *long-term* life goals. These are the important constants in your life. Your desire to thrive in each of these areas is something that will never go away. So it makes perfect sense that you will want to do something to nourish each of these categories every week of every year you live. And it makes perfect sense that items on your "to do" list that don't align with any of your categories aren't contributing to your long-term life desires. So, why do them? Don't panic yet—we'll talk more about that soon.

4) **Fill In Your "WANT TO DO" List**. Identify the high-level actions/projects/activities that need to be done in each of your categories for the upcoming week, and write them, bullet-point style, on your list under each category, leaving space between them so that they aren't all clumped together (both for ease of reading them and—spoiler alert—for what comes in Step 5). For example, for Career, I might bullet: client proposal, blog, and marketing. For Marriage: date night, weekly dinners. For Extended Family/Friends: birthday gifts, weekly connections. And for Personal Health: workouts, massage. Don't get bogged down in the detailed actions you need to take, just focus on the higher level. By keeping your initial focus on the higher level, you are freeing your subconscious mind to focus on the important things—not the urgent projects, the annoying people, or the items that *other* people think are important for you to have on your list. By focusing, you are staying grounded in *your* reality, confidently drawing boundaries around what truly will advance your life, not just what needs to be done today or tomorrow.

5) **List Your Tasks**. Now it's time to get into the detail. As I'm sure you have deduced, your tasks get listed under your high-level actions/projects/activities. These are the tasks that you need to complete *this week only* in order to move things forward. If your mind starts racing and you find that you are listing everything that needs to be done for the next few weeks, flip to the next page and you'll see I have a page titled "**FUTURE TO DO LIST**" ready for all of your thoughts. Record them there. *Do not* add tasks to your weekly "to do" list if they do not need to be done this week. If you do, you may start to feel overwhelmed and question your ability to accomplish everything in one week.

During this "to do" list exercise, the idea is to stay positively focused on furthering those things that are most important to you in your life and to look forward to a week of activity around each of those areas. The last thing we want is a turn to the negative, falling-off-a-cliff feeling, loaded with dread and anxiety for the week ahead. "To do" lists should be a celebration of all the wonderful things you are going to achieve this week that will make you healthy, wealthy, and loved. We want to avoid feeling that your "to do" list will make you grumpy, tired, overworked, and angry all week.

6) **Just One Piece of Paper!** So, what happens if you run out of room but still have tasks to add to your list? Most likely, the first tasks that came to mind—when you had plenty of room for writing—were the most important ones. The tasks you have left over are tasks that you think need to be done but that don't quite fit under your categories and high-level actions/projects/activities. I'd like you to turn to the next page in the back of the book and find a piece of paper ready to accept all of these misfit "to dos" titled "**LEFTOVER TO DO LIST**." Write down every task that you didn't have room for on your first piece of paper. You can organize by category if you'd like—that often makes things easier. This is the list of tasks that *you won't do*.

7) **Review Your Leftover "To Do" List**. Look at each task on your Leftover "To Do" list individually and ask yourself: Does this really need to be done by me?

The answer to that question is yes if—and only if—that task will make a profound difference in the progression of your categories. If the answer is yes, then you either need to prioritize it against something else you already have on your primary "to do" list and swap them, or add this to the list of things that can be done next week or in the future. I know that many times I feel a need to get everything done immediately, thinking that I can relax after I'm done. I have grown to feel comfortable with the idea that I will, hopefully, live a long life and every day of that life will be filled with something that needs to be done (including relaxing). So, whether it gets done this week or next, it will get done. Remember, this concept doesn't apply to every item. We have deadlines every day in both our professional and personal lives. So, focus on those deadlines week by week, and if you have a task that doesn't need to be done this week, just add it to the future task list.

Hopefully, however, the answer to your original question "Does this really need to be done by me?" is actually *no*. This is a much easier path. If the task does not need to be done by you, have someone else do it. Delegate, pay someone, or—if it's an unimportant task—just forget about it.

> ### *If you do not need to do a task, don't.*

Take a moment now—and each week as you create your "to do" list—to remind yourself of the following realities:

- You do not need to do everything. Nobody is expecting this feat of you except you.

- You are not as important as you think you are. Stop believing others are impacted (or angry) if you aren't at every meeting, on every phone call, or available 24/7.

- Delegating tasks to your team or your family helps them grow. The more they learn about what you do and how you do it, the more valuable they will be in their own careers/lives.

- Paying people to do household tasks helps others as much as it helps you. Plus, your ability to do the things that are most important to you is worth the money spent for a clean house/grocery delivery/etc.

- Overachieving in areas that aren't important to you takes time away from overachieving in areas that *are* important to you.

> *Living in balance requires us to discern what is important and needs to be done and to stop doing the rest.*

Say "Yes" to Happy and "No" to Struggle

Women and men think differently when it comes to saying "yes." I believe the need to say "yes" to everyone and everything is built into a woman's DNA. Women, for the most part, are people-pleasers and caregivers, reflecting how society has developed over hundreds (and thousands) of years. Some men also exhibit traits of people-pleasing, and many are primary caregivers, but most men still draw the line when it comes to prioritizing someone else's time and energy above their own. Women could learn a few lessons about the distinction between selfish and selfless from our male counterparts. Here's the first lesson: "Selfish" is not always a dirty word.

> *"Selfish" is not a dirty word.*

Everyone has responsibilities. We have obligations, commitments, and duties. We need social interaction to survive and thrive. We need to complete our projects and work responsibilities to earn wages to afford our lives. We have families, careers, plants, pets, communities, and other wonderful things in our lives that need to be nurtured through our time and energy.

But what many of us also possess is an unending desire to give all that we can to other people so that we will be accepted, praised, and viewed as being able to "do it all." We lack self-confidence, believing that one misplaced "no" will lead to the loss of a job, trust, or social standing.

Saying "yes" to everyone and everything else leaves minimal room for saying yes to yourself. When your daily life is filled with everyone else's priorities, it is no wonder there is no balance. Yet, to believe that other people are going to stop asking—or needing—us is crazy. It will never happen. The only course of action is to throw yourself into the mix right along with the other people who want something from you every day—and start saying "yes" to yourself.

Saying "yes" to yourself more often will make you a healthier person. Saying "yes" to myself meant that I was able to find time to eat healthier, exercise more, and sleep longer. Time normally spent saying "yes" to one last call for work, one more report for your boss, or one more committee meeting can instead be spent eating dinner with the family, reading a book to your children, taking a bubble bath, or playing a round of golf. The sheer act of saying "yes" to something that is a priority for you and letting go of something less important is the first step toward tipping your life scale back in your favor.

Okay. I'm sure we've talked enough about why it is important to say "yes" to yourself and "no" to others more often. I know you get it. You'll be happier, less stressed, healthier, and much more balanced. The hard part is *how* to say "yes" to ourselves more often when we are programmed with fear, guilt, and societal responsibility. Herein lies one of the hardest choices I'm going to ask you to make for yourself: the choice to be truly happy.

Our lives are surrounded by struggle. We are taught struggle in school, in church, from our parents, from the news, from almost any source that plays a part in defining what it takes to succeed. Even the work week is conducive to struggle—five days out of seven we work, receiving just two days of rest. In my corporate job, the mantra we all followed was: "Work Hard, Play Hard." The implication was that work always came before play—and both things were to be done "hard." We are conditioned to the idea that before we take time for ourselves, we have to finish whatever work needs to be done, whether that is in our careers or our personal lives.

The problem with this way of living is that the work is never done. How many of your recent work weeks have extended into your weekend? How many workdays have extended into work *nights*? How many "to do" lists have extended into "to do" novels? Struggle keeps us focused on getting more done in the hopes that, when finished, we will deserve time to do something we want to do. Unfortunately, that time never arrives.

Once you have made a conscious choice that you deserve to be happy, you have successfully defeated struggle. You have chosen to spend your time producing and contributing, not just working. You have chosen to spend your time nurturing and loving, not managing and controlling. You have chosen to spend your time feeling energized and free, not tired and trapped.

Once you have chosen to lead the life of a happy person, here are some practical approaches to putting yourself first:

- Take out your category list and review what you identified as your life priorities. The next time you are asked to do something that doesn't align with the development of any of these categories, don't say "yes" to the person asking. Tell them you are busy, help them delegate the job to someone more appropriate, or explain to them why something more important will suffer if you are required to spend your time working on their request. Working with someone to help find a solution to their problem usually yields a better result for everyone. Saying "yes" isn't always the best way to help others.

- Don't allow time you have set aside for your own personal use to be jeopardized. The classic example here is the giving up of time you set aside in your calendar to exercise. We all have good intentions, usually setting time aside each week to go to the gym, get outside for a run, or find some form of physical activity to keep healthy. This time is always the first to be given away when someone asks you to take a last-minute meeting, deal with a "fire drill," or cover for someone who is on vacation/out sick. Don't let your sacred time go. Yes, additional work may have to be done, but it should be done during your work time, not during your personal time. Find something else that week that can be moved into the next week, and replace this new development into that freed-up calendar space. Only you should set your priorities, and only you can ensure they remain your priorities.

- Do something for yourself each week that makes you happy, and enjoy yourself when you are doing it. Get a massage. Take a bubble bath. Play golf. Read a book. Do something that is for you, and only you. Enjoy time alone doing exactly what you want to be doing. Don't feel guilty about other people having to pick up some slack in order for you to have what you want. If they love you, they want you to be happy, and will appreciate being given the opportunity to help. Your colleagues and family will soon smarten up to the idea that the happier you are, the happier they will be.

> *Stop being the martyr, put aside the need to struggle,*
> *and make the decision to be happy.*

Two Important Four-Letter Words: PUSH BACK

Pushing back feels selfish. After all, doesn't everyone else have things that need to be done, too? Who are you to tell someone else that you can't do what they have asked simply because it doesn't fit nicely into your schedule? You know how busy your schedule is and you can only imagine that others—who have more children, bigger job responsibilities, or more community responsibilities—work even harder than you do.

Pushing back feels like you are skirting responsibility. If your boss comes to you with another meeting, another deliverable, or another project, how could you possibly say "no"? It's your job to receive work from your superior and get it done, right? At work, saying "no" could come at the high price of not being promoted, only getting a small raise, or not receiving a bonus at the end of the year.

Pushing back feels *mean*. There is something about the idea of saying "no" that makes us feel bad. "No" is a word associated with doing something wrong. How many times would your mother tell you, "I told you 'no,'" and you would hear the wrath in her voice? We frequently say "no" to the dog, the cat, the kids, our partners/spouses, but we seldom say "no" to the boss.

The idea of pushing back has received a pretty bad reputation over the years. People who push back aren't team players, they're avoiding responsibility, or they're self-centered. They are being rigid, unhelpful, and closed-minded. (I bet that, as you're reading this, even the thought of having to push back is creating a stressful, anxious response in you.) In fact, people who aren't used to pushing back probably spend more time stressing out about the *idea* of pushing back than the amount of time it would take to actually do the activity being requested.

So, let's take the phrase *push back* out of the "bad" category and reframe it into something constructive for both us and our recipients.

Let's say that it's Monday morning and you have started your week with a deluge of emails that needed attention yesterday. Monday morning moods are rampant in your household, as the kids are late for school and your partner/spouse has already left for work, leaving you with the breakfast dishes and the dog needing to be taken for a walk immediately.

You feel all right, though, because you have chosen this week to start your new exercise routine and are looking forward to the three hours you have booked (one hour each on Monday, Wednesday, and Friday mornings) to go for a long walk. Thinking about the fact that you have said "yes" to yourself makes you feel happy, relaxed, empowered, and ultimately more confident as you work toward a healthier life. Your exercise time will not only mean physical relief but mental relief as well, as you will get one full hour on each of those days to think your thoughts, listen to your music, or enjoy complete silence.

You get to the office and start to tackle that pile of emails from the weekend. Your heart sinks from your chest to your toes as you open one from your boss titled "Needed By Friday morning." As you open the email, you hope with all of your heart that whatever is needed by Friday is something that you have already started, which won't need a lot of work. Your week is full. There is no room for extra projects, regardless of the urgency. Thoughts of working late into the night start to increase your heart rate as the blood pumps more loudly in your ears. Your fingers ache with anxiety. You open the email.

Exactly as expected. A project needing urgent attention is awaiting your usual response: "Okay, I'll have it done by Friday." You start to think through your options and immediately find three hours of time that you can use to complete this new responsibility: the three hours you had set aside for exercising on Monday, Wednesday, and Friday. Appeasing yourself, you figure that maybe you can still stay committed to Friday's hour, as the project is due in the morning, but internally you know that will never happen, as you will need to use that hour to complete work you will have had to put aside to accommodate this urgent project.

Wait. As your heart beats faster and your hands get sweaty, stop for just one moment and take a deep breath. It's time for rational thinking to take over. Let's start with understanding your boss a little better.

We forget sometimes that our bosses are people, too. I know it may be hard to envision—especially if you have one who seems to notice every detail and sleeps just two hours a night—but yes, they are also people who have lives, interests outside of work, families, and commitments.

Our bosses are not mind-readers. Plus, chances are pretty good that you are actually one of many people your boss supervises. This, in addition to the fact that your boss reports to someone else and, therefore, also has an agenda, "to do" lists, and last-minute urgent projects, makes your boss just as human as you are.

So, before you start to get really pissed off at your boss for ruining your week with a last-minute urgent project, let's look at things from a different perspective.

Perhaps your boss:

- doesn't know what else is on your "to do" list this week;

- received this urgent project from someone up the food chain and wouldn't be able to complete it this week, so decided to delegate it to you;

- might not need *you* to do this project, but does need someone to get it done;

- has no idea what other commitments you have this week that might preclude you from getting this project done; or

- doesn't actually need the project done by Friday but was adding a few days' buffer to review the project.

There could be all sorts of other ideas you come up with, but the point is that changing your perspective for a moment will calm you down and give you the chance to look at some areas where you could push back.

Now it's time to re-engage that confidence you found in Chapter Two. Breathe deeply a few times and remind yourself that you, and only you, are the person in charge of your life.

You—only you—are in charge of your life.

Pushing back in a professional environment takes poise, respect, and common sense. You possess all of these characteristics, so now is the time to use them. Depending on the mode of communication your boss is most receptive to (email, phone call, scheduled meeting, etc.), either craft an email, place the phone call, or schedule a quick meeting. *Now.* Don't put things off by finishing the rest of your emails and stewing about the fact that your week is ruined. Get to your boss quickly so that the two of you have time to work through your options, ideas, and alternatives sooner rather than later.

This is the time to be honest. Open up to your boss and make it known that it will be very difficult to get the project done by Friday due to the task load you are already carrying for the week. Remember, your boss most likely has no idea what you do during your working hours. In fact, your boss most likely doesn't realize how many hours a day you work. You do not have to give up the information that you have three hours scheduled to exercise. This is your right. Don't feel guilty. Stop giving up your personal time for work.

Suggest to your boss that you can get the project done by Monday (if that is doable), or that something else may not get done this week if you must complete the new project; ask if you can delegate the project, or other work you have, to a teammate; or simply ask if the project can wait until a later time when you have the time to do it properly. I always end this kind of email/conversation with a reminder to my boss that I really want to do the best I can and deliver quality work on both my current responsibilities *and* this additional work, but to complete the new project under the current timeframe would result in subpar quality.

In the over-scheduled, fast-paced, multitasked world we live in, we too often replace quantity with quality. Don't let that happen—and be sure your boss knows that you don't want it to happen on your watch.

At this point, more often than not, your boss will react positively, and between the two of you, you'll figure out some way to keep your boundaries sacred while making arrangements for getting the project done. If, for some unfortunate reason, your boss doesn't budge, take a deep breath and refocus on your calendar. Initiating change is difficult and your resolve will often be tested—this is the standard process for creating a new habit.

I implore you to stay strong and continue to live in the new reality you have created. Don't cancel your personal plans/time to free up a few extra hours. Instead, think about all of the work-related commitments you have and try to eliminate one or more of those. Look to meetings that you may not need to attend, or phone calls which could be shortened. Find items that are not urgent and reschedule them for the next week. You can also reduce the time you spend on email every day. Respond to the important items (these would be emails from your boss) but refrain from responding to other emails that are less important. You can clean those up next week, but this week, they are not necessary. (They may not even be necessary next week.)

The idea of pushing back also works for meetings you are being asked to attend that coincide with time you have booked for your own priorities. Instead of responding with your usual "yes," try responding with "I already have something scheduled at that time, is it possible for us to find a different time for this call/meeting? Perhaps later in the day or the next day at the same time?" You do not have to tell anyone what is on your schedule. Offering alternatives demonstrates that you are serious about the meeting and want to ensure you can attend. Many times you will be surprised to find that the alternative times you suggest are better for others as well, and they will appreciate that you were bold enough to push back.

Yes, sometimes you will have to sacrifice your personal time for something important at work. That's part of being a professional, enjoying your work, and advancing your career. But you do not need to sacrifice all the time. Pushing back is not the same as saying "no." It's simply a way to open up the lines of communication with a fellow human being and work together to come up with a better solution—for everyone.

The Big "E"

The ego. What an amazing part of every human being. Unlike an arm or a leg or any other actual physical part of our bodies, our ego is simply an opinion we have of ourselves. This opinion rests in our minds and controls the way we view ourselves in relation to our surroundings. One day we are convinced we are the smartest person in the room and the next day we might wonder how we ever managed to get dressed without help.

Our ego can bring us to great heights—in our careers, in the way we present ourselves to the world through our physical appearance, and in our lives overall. Our ego can also talk us down, make us feel insignificant or stupid, timid or ashamed. Our egos stand in the way of living in balance because they preach a never-ending sermon of how important we are to our jobs, how if we screw something up in our jobs we may no longer have a job, and that being irreplaceable in our jobs is a desirable state. The pressure inevitably results in working too many hours, answering too many emails, attending too many meetings, and volunteering for too many additional responsibilities.

So, as we work toward new balance, I'm going to do you a favor and tell you some inconvenient truths about yourself in relation to your career. Put your ego and emotions aside for a moment and read these truths as they are intended—as unbiased, nonjudgmental facts. These are not intended to insult you or put you down. However, if they hit a nerve, we might be onto something.

- **You are not as important—or needed—as you think you are at work.** While people need you, rely on you, and think you do great work, if you were not at work, someone else would be doing your job. Apple is still a very successful company without Steve Jobs. Every four to eight years, we get a new president. Life will always go on, even without us. I realize that—on some level—this can sound scary to those who don't want someone else doing their job. Let go of that emotion for a moment by reminding yourself that you are capable of getting another job. You got this far once, you can do it again.

- **Other people are just as smart as, if not smarter than, you.** Sure, you are smarter than some people as well, but that doesn't mean you have to solve every problem, create every new product, or have the best idea in every meeting. The more you allow others to collaborate by adding their knowledge and ideas to the mix, the better the work product will become overall.

- **You aren't the only one who can answer questions.** Your boss and/or client doesn't always need you to answer her question—she just needs *someone* who can answer the question. The important thing here is that the question gets answered or the problem gets solved, not who answers or solves it. You will not be viewed as unimportant, unintelligent, or unresponsive if you are unable to answer every question. People are much more interested in getting a quick, quality answer to their question or problem than they are in knowing who actually delivered the goods.

- **Asking others to complete work that you cannot do is not a sign of weakness.** In fact, it's a sign of a well-developed leader who understands her own time and brain capacity limitations. Additionally, the delegation of work is the only way that you will develop a functioning team.

- **Pay attention to what matters.** You will be remembered for the impact that you had on your family, friends, and environment, not how much work you got done.

- **Being busy does not make you important—nor does it prove your worth.** And spending time telling other people how busy you are is a waste of time— both yours and theirs.

- **Saving vacation time won't make you live longer.** Bragging about how much vacation time you have left at the end of the year says more about your priorities than it does your performance. Sitting in your office every day does not make you important.

Set your ego aside. Stop defining yourself by how much work you complete in a day. Start paying more attention to your teammates and peers to understand how you can rely on each other to work less and produce more as a team.

> *You cannot define your worth by how much work you complete in a day.*

Put aside the notion that you are indispensable—or stop worrying that you *might be* indispensable—and see what happens when you take a day off and let others answer questions, attend meetings, and put out fires. Delegate work to others, allowing them to learn and grow.

One of my favorite "Ego Exercises" is the two-week vacation. To many, the idea of a two-week vacation is akin to an alien from outer space—it just doesn't exist. However, the two-week vacation is the most logical and practical way to put your ego in check while taking a big step toward rebalancing your work/life ratio.

Why is a two-week vacation more important than a one-week vacation? There are three important factors that make a one-week vacation an ego *supporter*. First, people will easily wait a week for you to come back to solve a problem, answer an email, or attend a meeting. One week is not a lot of time, so instead of finding another person to fill in while you are gone, people will simply wait for your return. Then, on the Monday morning of your return, they will bombard you with their problems and expect immediate resolutions—after all, in their minds, they have already waited a week for your answers.

Secondly, if shit does hit the fan during your one-week vacation, no one will hesitate to call you. Our society has lost respect for the one-week vacation, assuming that you are not far enough away from work to require longer vacation time.

Therefore, there is an unwritten assumption that you aren't completely unplugged—which is usually reinforced by the fact that you most likely *are* reading emails on a regular basis to "keep things moving" while you are out. When we believe that being away from work for one week will have an impact on the flow of production, others will believe it as well, and ensure that you are never too far away.

Lastly, taking a one-week vacation sends the message to our bodies and minds that we do not need downtime; that we are superhuman, physically and mentally, and require little to no regeneration. Let's be realistic—the amount of rest and relaxation you get in a one-week vacation is basically non-existent. The week prior to vacation we work even harder than we normally would to ensure we get as much done as possible prior to leaving. By the time we leave, we're exhausted. The first few days of vacation usually entail traveling or a variety of social engagements. On day three or four, you begin to unwind a bit and enjoy yourself a little. But, by day five, you are starting to stress about going back to work because you know how the first week back to work after vacation goes: Everyone who waited for your return will bombard you with deadlines for issues that are now urgent, your unread email count will easily be in the triple digits, and your guilty conscience will make you feel as if you need to work double time to make up for being away for the week. If you make it to day six, you will start to believe that things have collapsed without you at work and day seven is spent catching up on emails to ensure that you hit the ground running on Monday morning.

Alternately, you can choose to put your ego aside and enjoy a wonderful two-week vacation. This will require asking others to help cover for you, admitting that you are prioritizing time away from work over time at work, realizing that you might miss an important meeting (there will be others), and worst of all, acknowledging that things might actually go well while you are out. *Oh no!*

People won't wait for you to get back to solve their problems. They will either solve them themselves or seek out other help. Teammates may grow and learn to help manage while you are out, and realize they can do things that are usually done by you. Even your email inbox will probably be smaller than after taking a one-week vacation, because people will have figured out how to move on without you.

Above all else—and sometimes much more difficult in the realm of ego taming—is the message you send to your own mind and body. When you take a two-week vacation, you are admitting to yourself that you can't do it all. You *do* need time away. Sleep, relaxation, and time spent laughing and loving with your family and friends seems like soft stuff, but it is the stuff that your life's longevity is built around. The age-old adages that you'll sleep when you die or that you'll enjoy life when you retire were developed by people with big egos. For those less worried about constantly proving themselves to others at work, sleeping and enjoying life should happen every day.

Upon returning from my first two-week vacation, I was called into my supervisor's office. For a fleeting moment, I believed that the company had gotten along so well without me that she was going to tell me that they no longer needed me. She took a deep breath, sat back in her chair with her arms crossed, and asked me if I had had a good time. I couldn't hold back the Cheshire cat smile that slowly filled my face. She smiled back and then simply said, "You were missed."

A two-week vacation can be exactly what you need to remind everyone how great you really are.

Practically, the key to taking two weeks off is in the art of writing your Out Of Office (OOO) reply. The OOO is the email, or phone message, that tells people what to do, where to go, or whom to talk to in your absence. There is a right way of creating an OOO—and there is a wrong way. The wrong way is to let people know that you are "out of the office but will be checking emails periodically and will respond when [you]

have a moment." Or, my favorite passive ego-fee
be checking my emails, but if your matter is urg
call me on my mobile phone." You might as well sε
vacation, and I can live without you, but I know yoι
without me, so here's how to contact me." In both of these
cases, people will contact you with items that are not urgent
because, in our fast-paced corporate society, everything is
deemed "urgent."

A well-written OOO that earns you two fairly peaceful
weeks of rest and relaxation reads as follows: "Thank you for
your email/phone call. I am out of the office on vacation until
[date]. If this is an urgent matter, please call Sam Support at
555-1212 and he will direct you to someone who can help
you. Thank you."

This simple statement is fantastic on multiple dimensions:

1. You start with a pleasantry — everyone likes to be
   thanked for writing/calling.

2. You do not apologize for being out of the office on
   vacation. In fact, you are up front about where you
   are. I like to believe that people, at the core, are nice.
   And, for that reason, if someone knows you are on
   vacation, they will be less likely to interrupt you. Also,
   you are setting a great example for others — if you can
   take two weeks of vacation and tell people, you might
   inspire more people to do the same thing.

3. You give your writer/caller an option. You help them
   solve their problem by giving them someone else to
   contact. You have given them a solution to the "problem" that you are out of the office.

4. Ending your OOO message with a simple thank you
   leaves no expectation that you will respond to every
   contact. So often we create expectations that we will
   respond, which then root themselves in our psyche so
   that our guilt-ridden consciousness feels the need to

respond to even the most benign email. This is a waste of time and, frankly, creates more work for both you and the person you are responding to. So just don't tell people you will respond to them. Don't set that expectation. When you come back from vacation, you will determine if you need to respond and, if so, you will. If you come back from vacation and determine that you do not need to respond for whatever reason (i.e., the deadline passed, you don't have valuable insights to lend, or the issue was resolved ten emails further down in your queue), then you won't feel guilty about just deleting the email and never thinking about it again.

Putting together a well-written, definitive, pleasant OOO message that includes where to go if someone needs urgent help (reminder: this is *not* your mobile phone) is without a doubt the most important skill one can master for a peaceful two weeks away. Lose the ego, hand off to others, and don't feel guilty about not responding when you return. If the issue wasn't urgent, no one will notice. If the issue was urgent, someone else probably already took care of it.

You are loved. You are needed. You are wanted. By your family. You are much more important to your family than you are to your boss. If your ego needs a stroke, be there for someone you love, not someone you work for.

> *You matter more to your family than you do to your boss.*

Judgment, Worry, and Meeting Expectations

Only the mentally strongest among us can detach themselves from caring what other people think. The rest of us worry constantly about whether we are living up to others' expectations.

We are so attached to our desired outcomes that we worry about things we cannot control and judge ourselves and our abilities against unrealistic expectations—expectations we believe were set by others but which really only exist in our own ego-driven minds.

A day spent not judging your, or other people's, actions—and of remaining worry-free in the face of uncertainty—is a day spent in balance. On a day like this, your stress is low, your work product is exceptional, and your time spent with your family is fully lived. Visually, when I think of a day of no judgment, worry, or working to meet others' expectations, I think of a Buddhist monk, sitting in maroon robes, chanting mantra meditations. Not a care in the world, no one to impress, and a peace of mind so anchored in detachment that he floats through the universe.

Nope, this type of day is not anything that would ever land on my calendar.

This is perhaps the hardest yet most powerful of all of the steps to rebalancing your life. Letting go of our compulsion to conform, impress, and control is a scary proposition. But to not do so is to stay a slave to always working harder than needed.

Think for a moment of some of the greatest leaders of our world. Gandhi. Martin Luther King, Jr. Steve Jobs. Or people you may know who have quit their jobs to pursue their dreams. Perhaps you even know someone whom you admire simply because she lives her life on her terms and does not care what anyone else thinks. There is no shortage of hard work for people who live their lives to the fullest; the difference is that they are controlling the full expression of their lives. Your goal needs to be more than just making a living; it needs to include enjoying what you do, how you do it, when you do it, and why you do it.

But this book is a *realist's* guide to less work and more life, so with all due respect to the philosophical and spiritual, let's talk about how to *realistically* let go of judgment, worry, and the need to meet other people's expectations.

It all starts with understanding *why you do what you do*. These are similar to your "Whys" identified in the previous chapter, but they are more action oriented. For example, career may be one of your "Whys," but why is it? Why do you work? Why do you choose to work doing the job you are doing? Why do you spend time with the people whom you choose to spend time with? Why do you eat the food you eat? Why do you dress the way you dress?

Ask the question "why" about anything you do and take the time to write down your answers—you'll find an empty page titled "**WHY DO I DO WHAT I DO?**" for your musing in the back of the book. You can use your "Why and What" list as a starting point, but really get to the nitty-gritty of everything that you do. Think about how you spend your day and ask yourself "why." Be honest with yourself as you answer. Don't worry about others reading what you have written and judging, laughing at, or blaming you for any of your answers. This is an exercise in self-awareness, and to do it right, you must put aside caring about anything but yourself and how you feel.

You may not succeed in creating a complete definition of your *whys* during your first time through this exercise, so I encourage you to do it regularly for a few weeks. The more you can succinctly define your *whys*, the more strongly you will feel about who you are, thus the easier it will become to deflect judgment, eliminate worry, and strive only to meet your own goals. Through the articulation of your *whys*, you will draw the strength needed to chart your own life course, draw your boundaries, and live your life in your own defined balance.

Now, let's think about a day at work. The typical office bureaucracy consistently leaves us wondering, how do others perceive me? Am I someone who is seen as capable? Do I socialize with the right people who can help take my career further? Do others in higher positions view me as valuable?

Worry trips over the heels of judgment. The project that is due, the last email you sent to your boss's boss, the meeting behind closed doors that you weren't invited to, the nonresponse to an email you sent, which has you worried that someone has taken offense or doesn't like your work. The angst you feel after a presentation when it was obvious not everybody in the room agreed with your point of view. We worry about things that are outside of our control and assume immediately that the answer, reaction, response, or judgment of others will be negative.

Lastly, we wrap our days up in striving to meet the expectations of others. We're not always clear on what those expectations are, however, and many times we impose our expectations on ourselves but tell ourselves that the expectations belong to other people. Did I talk enough in the meeting? Was my report written well enough? Did I clean the house/cook dinner/help the kids with their homework enough? Any question you ask yourself about your abilities that ends with "well enough" is a product of attempting to meet the expectations of others.

Now, let's apply your *whys* to your day. For each *why* scenario, act with the confidence of knowing *why* it is that you do what you do, and you'll find that the judgment, worry, and striving to meet others' expectations start to melt away. They no longer matter. What does matter is *why*. If someone doesn't like you, who cares, as long as you are making forward steps toward your *why*? If completing the project, sending the email, or doing your presentation were all stepping stones to achieving your *why*, then stop worrying about anything extraneous. If you can answer the question "Did I do things that aligned with my *why*?" with a yes, then meeting the expectations of others is meaningless.

My first job in the corporate world was as a technology consultant. My human resources career started three years into my consulting career. At the time, moving from a client-facing role to an administrative role was not a choice many people made. I did it because I wanted to help other new consultants build careers based on quality work and an understanding of the corporate environment—two concepts I felt were lacking when I first started out. I had a very successful human resources career because I always put the person I was helping first, the job second.

As I continued to climb up the ladder of success, I experienced promotions, awards, and a comfortable bank account. I also experienced burnout, a quickly vanishing personal life, and ten pounds of unwanted stress around the middle of my stomach. I spent my days responding to the priorities, moods, and egos of those I reported to, losing sight of the needs of the people I was representing. My energy was sapped, my mood atrocious, and my calendar booked with meetings about budgets, policies, and procedures. It wasn't long before my performance suffered and the worst thing that could happen happened: my annual performance rating read "Consistent With Peers."

Average? I was *average*? This was the last straw. After a week-long pity party, I picked myself up, dusted myself off, and took out my journal. At the top of the page, in capital letters, I wrote "My WHYs" and proceeded to write down everything in my life that made me happy. I knew something was truly my *why* as I wrote it because I felt relaxed, happy, and expansive, instead of stressed out and constricted. I wrote from my heart, not my head. I included personal, professional, and emotional items. This exercise reminded me why I had gotten into human resources in the first place: to help people.

This anchoring to my career *why* was the very reason I left my corporate job and started my Executive Health and Leadership coaching business. There was no shortage of people who thought I was crazy, irrational, and "throwing it all away." I let them judge me. I accepted the fact that I wasn't meeting *their* expectations of what I should do with my life, and I stopped worrying about what they thought. Sure, I was scared, but I was deeply routed in why I love to work, and I wasn't going to deviate from that for anyone. I now get called brave, focused, goal oriented, strong, and yes, I still get called crazy! While those terms feel better, they still are just other people's opinions. What truly makes me smile is when a client tells me that I've made a difference in their lives. I'd rather stress about helping someone than stress about what people think of me helping someone.

> *Wouldn't you rather worry about helping someone than worry about what people think of you helping someone?*

Defining who we are, why we are here, and how we want to live gives us the strength and focus to control our actions and reactions. Taking control of our actions and reactions helps build the mental strength needed to detach from judgment, worry, and meeting expectations. It is this detachment that opens up the space and time needed to rebalance your life.

Chapter 4

Better Health, Better Life

Anything in balance has a centering mechanism. Think back on pictures you've seen of the scales used for weighing gold, animals, spices, or food—before everything was electronic. Scales of this kind had two arms that connected into a centering base. If you weighted the scale too heavily on one side, the other side would rise, requiring you to remove items from the heavy side or add items to the other side until you struck the right balance and both arms of the scale hovered at the same height. Back and forth, back and forth, the arms would move as you experimented to find just the right amount of weight to keep the scale in balance. The center, however, never moved. It stayed grounded, holding up the scale's arms, never leaning to one side or the other.

Your health is the center of your life's scale. Career, family, community, and other responsibilities in your life get loaded on the arms of your life's scale. Back and forth, up and down, the arms of the scale move to accommodate the urgency, necessity, or desire of your life's commitments. But what's holding your scale in place? Hopefully, it is being anchored by a center that is strong enough to hold the scale upright, while responding to your constant attempts to find balance.

Health is not just a physical attribute. Yes, eating well and exercising are the basics to maintaining a healthy weight, looking your best, warding off disease, and aging gracefully. However, good health is much more than all of that. Good health also includes being happy, sleeping well, lowering your stress, raising your awareness, achieving mindfulness, creating loving relationships, and feeling a sense of contribution to the world around us.

And you thought it was hard just to eat better and exercise more! Now you have to be happy, sleep eight hours every night, meditate, and find some way of feeding all of the hungry people in the world. I can feel your stress mounting. Take a deep breath. I'm happy to tell you that creating a holistic, healthy center is actually quite easy and requires very little additional time or resources. In fact, the only requirement is a commitment to try at least one of the following practical recommendations.

When you begin to see how well it works, with fairly little effort, I suspect your desire to continue through all of the recommendations will increase, resulting in your better health. Your healthy center will then be prepared to support the rest of your life, in balance.

You Are What (and When) You Eat

To remain living, we must eat food and drink water in regular intervals. There, I have successfully consolidated all science, diet theories, and nutritional concepts down into the most important piece of information to know about eating and drinking: You must do both regularly. Let's now explore the easiest and healthiest ways to provide your body with food and water.

WHEN YOU EAT

When's the last time you were hungry? Do you remember how you felt? Was your attention drawn from participating in a meeting to focusing on the gnawing emptiness in your belly? Did your mind wander from answering your emails to wondering when and where your next meal would come from? Did your otherwise good mood turn abrupt and nasty? Was the idea of taking a quick nap suddenly the best idea you have ever had? Did you experience a headache, stomachache, or an annoying increase in the amount of saliva in your mouth?

Hunger can turn any high-performing, energized, well-balanced professional into a nonfocused, belligerent, drooling, lethargic professional. Hunger has the ultimate control over your ability to function as a well-balanced human being. Being hungry is never a good idea, for you or the people around you.

I'll share a personal story about my own Jekyll and Hyde tendencies. I like to consider myself a fairly well-balanced, healthy individual who often has a smile on her face and a skip in her step, and is pretty enjoyable to be around. Not that I don't have my moments—we all do—but if you were to sum me up in three words, I've heard they would most likely be "healthy, happy, and free." I attribute my healthy, happy, free living to many things, one of the most important of which is regular access to food.

On occasion, my ability to plan my meals and deliver food to my body on a regular basis is derailed. Whether we are confronted with unexpected errands that need immediate attending to or a spouse who doesn't have the same eating requirements we do—and sees nothing wrong with another hour before dinner—life happens to us all. The best-laid eating plans can fall apart pretty quickly, sometimes leaving me just plain hungry. When that happens, the best recommendation is for those around me to take cover, because it's "Feed the Bitch Time."

"Feed the Bitch Time" is a phrase my husband affectionately coined to describe that point in time when my hunger has taken over my otherwise pleasant demeanor and replaced it with, yes, a bitch. And, no, I have never taken offense to this phrase—because it is entirely true.

During the peak of Feed the Bitch Time, my stomach feels as if I have swallowed a drill and it's boring a hole straight through my bellybutton from the front of my body to the back. My head feels as though with just a sneeze, I could potentially blow my brains right out my eyeballs. I have no patience for anything or anyone. Everyone annoys me. Ask me a question and I'll bark back an answer that sounds like, "I don't know, I can't process anything at the moment because I'm too hungry." I get angry, frustrated, annoyed, and just plain bitchy.

Eating regularly keeps your energy levels up, feeds a positive approach to your everyday life, and protects your family and friends from experiencing your monster alter ego. But it's not always easy to plan full meals around busy schedules. So, in lieu of three square meals a day, here are some easy ways to make sure you are feeding your body on a regular basis:

- **Carry snacks.** A purse, backpack, computer bag, or briefcase can be a perfect place to hide healthy snacks. Even deep coat pockets will suffice. The next time you are at the store, buy a few boxes of granola bars (preferably with no added sugar or corn syrup), premade bags of trail mix (a combination of nuts, dried fruits, seeds, and sometimes chocolate-covered goodies), dried fruit, and/or nuts. Then, put a few bars and small bags of your newfound treats into your bags, your coat pockets, your car, your office drawers—you get the idea. Wherever you find some storage space, fill it up with some snacks. When you are packing for a business trip, bring some bars/bags with you in your suitcase. Heading from work to your kid's sports game or dance recital? Open up the glove compartment and there's a healthy alternative to not eating dinner. Too busy to eat a good breakfast this morning? Grab a granola bar and run out the door.

- **Double your dinner preparation and eat the leftovers for lunch.** Having a premade lunch has multiple healthy benefits. First, homemade meals are usually healthier than buying from a store, cafeteria, or restaurant. Second, eating homemade meals is better for your financial health than having to buy your lunch. Third, you don't have to make a special trip to go get lunch—it will be sitting, waiting for you, either in the refrigerator at home or in the office. And, chances are good that if you have food waiting for you, you will eat it instead of skipping a meal.

- **Learn your way around the closest vending machine, convenience store, or airport kiosk.** When we are busy working, managing families, and travelling, eating tends to take a back seat. However, there are a surprising number of healthy snacks found in vending machines, convenience stores, and airport kiosks. Before your next meeting, in between child drop-offs and pick-ups, or on your way to catch a flight, take a second and grab some nuts, dried fruit, or granola bars (found in all three locations). A small offering to your stomach in between important commitments will ensure that you show up engaged, energized, and ready for the next challenge.

WHAT YOU EAT

Not all food is created equal when it comes to strengthening your body and mind. There are some foods that contribute to building strong bones and muscles (including our brains), managing a healthy weight, reducing the chance of illness and disease, and generally making us look and feel better, both now and as we grow older. There are other foods that reduce our muscle and bone strength, contribute to gaining weight, increase the chance of illness and disease, and make us look and feel lethargic, angry, and old.

The trick is to eat the foods in the first category, which means filling your body with whole foods.

Whole foods are defined as "foods that have been processed or refined as little as possible and are free from additives or other artificial substances." Basically, the closer a unit of food is to its natural state, the more "whole" it is. An apple, for example, is grown on a tree, picked, then consumed. An apple is a whole food. Fresh fruits and vegetables are whole foods. Fish, chicken, beef, and pork are all whole foods. Eggs are a whole food. Grains such as brown rice and quinoa are whole foods.

As the definition notes, there can be a varying range on the whole food scale, since "as little processing as possible" could mean many different things. For example, white rice is a whole food, but due to the nature of how it is processed, brown rice is a *better* whole food. When brown rice is processed, only the husk is removed. In processing white rice, however, the bran is removed (which is what gives you the healthy dose of fiber in brown rice), and then the white rice is also usually polished and precooked.

Once you start to consider where the food you buy comes from, it becomes pretty easy to sort the whole foods from the processed. Take a look at the next meal you eat and break it down into its whole food components versus its overly processed parts. Or, take inventory of your shopping cart the next time you are in a grocery store and see if you can spot what is whole and what is overly processed—or even fake. Hint: The more ingredients you find on the packaging, the more processed or fake the food.

At face value, eating whole foods versus overly processed/fake foods seems to be a no-brainer, but have you ever considered why? We all learned this in our high school nutrition classes, but it bears reviewing for those of us who have forgotten those valuable lessons from our past. (Note: I am not a nutritionist, so the following Nutrition 101 review will be done in simple, easy to understand terms—the only way I know how to describe these things.)

The human body functions at its best when it is clean, full of nutrients, and able to find—from the foods we eat—what it needs for strong muscle, bone, and brain development. Whole foods naturally contain only what the body needs—no more and no less. They have not been unduly processed and therefore do not include anything unnatural, nor do they exclude anything natural that might be needed by your body. During digestion, whole foods are easily broken down into their basic parts: proteins, carbohydrates, and nutrients. These proteins, carbohydrates, and nutrients are then sent throughout the body to where they are needed most. This process leaves nothing in the body that the body doesn't know what to do with—everything is stripped, used, then cleaned out of the body.

Overly processed/fake foods, on the other hand, leave behind chemicals and other additives that your body doesn't know how to handle. Our bodily functions were developed hundreds of thousands of years ago when we evolved into the human body form. We were never made to digest the chemicals that we put into our bodies in our modern era, as they didn't exist in the world at that time. Anything we ingest that our body doesn't know how to use gets either stored or, if we are lucky, eliminated. It is the stuff that has been stored that slowly, over time, appears to us as additional weight, or bone and muscle disease. In parallel, the lack of nutrients, proteins, and carbohydrates manifest as disease of your organs, underdeveloped physical and mental abilities, and reduced longevity.

It comes down to this: If you are what you eat, would you rather be an abundant farmland or a chemical plant?

> *You are what you eat. Would you rather be a nature preserve or a bag of chemical preservatives?*

The food we eat not only impacts our physical health, it has a major bearing on our emotional health as well. Food directly impacts our moods and our energy levels, heightens our awareness to what's happening in our immediate circle of influence, and elevates our intelligence. Because whole foods provide us the proteins, carbohydrates, and nutrients needed to sustain a healthy body, eating them will tend to keep your energy levels consistent, put you in a positive frame of mind, reduce your stress levels, keep you focused on the important events happening in your life, and allow you to think and create at intensified levels.

What happened to you during the last meeting you attended? Did you start looking for a source of caffeine around two o'clock? How did you feel at four o'clock when the urge to take a cookie from the middle of the table overwhelmed any other thought in your mind? Purposefully notice how you feel, act, and participate when your body has eaten a regular, whole, and healthy diet. You'll like what you find out about yourself.

You can find whole foods almost everywhere. In the airport, at your meetings, out at restaurants, in gas station snack shops and, yes, even in vending machines. Saying it is impossible to find whole foods is no longer an excuse for anyone. Trail mixes are found in all airports, vending machines, and snack shops. Salads and whole proteins can be found in restaurants and sandwich shops, and where whole grains may not be as accessible, there is always the baked potato or whole wheat alternative. I know, eating an apple as your afternoon snack is nowhere near as appealing as a cookie, but the way it helps you feel and perform for the rest of the day will change your mind forever.

Unfortunately, whole foods sound intimidating to many people. Where will I find them? How will I prepare them? Aren't they more expensive than processed foods because they are healthy and fresh? Let me give you a few of my favorite tricks when it comes to finding, preparing, and buying whole foods.

I'm not one to spend a lot of time or money shopping for—or preparing—healthy food, so I pretty much promise success for anyone who tries these tricks.

- **When you go to the grocery store, shop only in the aisles around the perimeter of the store.** The perimeter of the grocery store is generally where you find the fresh or dried fruits, vegetables, meats, fish, freshly baked breads, nuts, and seeds. When you venture into the middle of the store, you become surrounded by aisles of boxed food, usually with expiration dates months in the future, indicating the use of unnatural life-extending ingredients. There are exceptions, of course, but if eighty percent of your cart is filled with food from the perimeter of the grocery store, you are probably doing well in eating a whole foods diet.

- **Frozen fruits and vegetables are just as healthy as—and often much less expensive than—fresh fruits and vegetables.** In fact, frozen fruits/vegetables are sometimes healthier, for you *and* our environment, than fresh fruits/vegetables. Fruits and vegetables that have been frozen have been picked at the height of their freshness and immediately frozen, freezing in all of the nutrients, whereas fresh fruits/vegetables are not always that fresh. Many times fruits/vegetables, like berries, bananas, melons, peaches, avocados, green beans, and broccoli, have been picked before full ripeness (not allowing the nutrients in the food to fully mature), then flown halfway around the world to sit on a grocery store shelf while they ripen. Grocery stores want to sell their inventory, so often these fruits and vegetables sit far past their peak of ripeness, again impacting their nutrient density (not to mention their taste). Here's a rule of thumb: If a fruit or vegetable is not in season in your geographic area (or within a few hundred miles of your geographic area), eating the frozen version will probably be healthier and less expensive. And, for those environmental enthusiasts, buying frozen "out of season" vegetables is more "green" as well, since you save all of the jet fuel used to bring the "fresh" fruits and vegetables in from the other side of the world. Frozen fruits and vegetables usually require only a few minutes of microwaving or defrosting before serving; it doesn't get much easier than that.

- **Cooking can be faster than ordering in.** You can bake a piece of chicken and microwave some frozen spinach and a "baked" potato in less time than it will take you to order and pick up a pizza from your nearest pizza parlor. Try it some night. Time yourself in both scenarios, and see which one takes you less time. Bake the chicken with a fun spice blend you can pick up in the seasonings section of the grocery store, toss the spinach with a little garlic and olive oil, and put a dollop of Greek yogurt on your baked potato, and you'll not only have a healthy meal, but a flavor extravaganza. Pizza? Who wants pizza when you can have a gourmet chicken dinner in the same amount of time?

WHAT YOU DRINK

Water is the "whole food" of liquids. It is a compound composed of one part oxygen and two parts hydrogen. No preservatives, no fake colors, no extra flavoring or sugars. Just oxygen and hydrogen in a liquid state.

Water is a necessity for good physical health. Water makes our skin glow, our hair shine, and our waistlines smaller. Water helps eliminate toxins from our bodies and keeps our systems working fluidly (pun intended). Water prevents dehydration, reduces headaches and migraines, relieves fatigue, regulates body temperature, and even reduces bad breath.

Water is also essential for good mental health. Water gives you energy (oxygen is a natural pick-me-up), lightens your mood, and helps your brain think more clearly. Who wouldn't want to have high energy, be in a good mood, and ooze brilliance every day?

So, knowing the benefits of water for your physical and mental health, why is it that we don't all drink more water? Is it because we don't have time to get up and get water from the water cooler/cafeteria/refrigerator? Or is it because we don't like the taste—or we want something that actually *has* a taste? Is it because, the more we drink, the more we will need to get up and go to the bathroom? If we're being honest, most people don't drink water regularly because they are addicted to some other form of liquid—usually soda.

For those who find it "hard" to drink more water due to access or taste, here are a few ideas for you.

- **Plan ahead.** Every night before you go to bed, put a full glass of water on your bedside table. In the morning, sometime between getting out of bed and putting on your clothes, drink that entire glass of water. Boom. The water will immediately wake you up, give you energy, and help you think more clearly (even more than a cup of coffee), and will count toward your overall water goal for the day. All within the first thirty minutes of being awake.

- **Carry on.** Invest in an easy-to-carry water bottle and fill it once in the morning before you go to work, once at lunchtime, and once as you leave your office. This water bottle approach eliminates the need to get up and get more water throughout the day, as you are filling your bottle at times when you would normally be up and moving around (even though getting up and walking to the water cooler is a great way to get some additional exercise).

- **Create your own flavored water.** This is one of my favorite tricks. Fill a pitcher with water and add sliced lemons, limes, oranges, or any other fruits that you like. You can add just one fruit or mix flavors for more fun. Keep this pitcher in your refrigerator within easy reach and refill your glass as much as desired. The bonus here is that you will also drink in some nutrients from the fresh fruit.

- **Keep it sparkly**. If you need something fizzy, try drinking seltzer or sparkling water (flavored or unfla-vored—but with no sugar). Many people I know who are trying to shed the soda habit need something that "feels like" they are drinking soda, and the carbonation helps fool your brain.

- **Remember: Walking is good for you.** For those who do not like the additional trips to the bathroom, I will remind you of the benefits of moving away from your desk/computer on a regular basis (your eyes and brain need the break), the physical activity of walking to the bathroom (those steps count), and the benefits of flushing bad stuff out of your body.

Eating whole foods and drinking water on a regular basis will help to create a healthy body and mind. A body and mind that will feel energized, alive, in focus, strong, vibrant, peaceful, and balanced. A body that is attractive, able to easily move from one place to another, rise to challenges, and play with children. A mind that is clear, strategic, creative, thoughtful, and alert. If you can achieve these things with your body and mind, imagine how that will then impact your overall life.

Feeding your body is feeding your life. After all, your life will never be in balance if you're dead.

> *If you do nothing else:* Try the water by your bedside trick listed above. Drinking more water is the best place to start when overhauling your eating/drinking habits. Once you have created this new morning habit, move on to eating more whole foods.

Stop Sitting on Your Butt

Chances are good that if you are reading this book right now, you have successfully created a full life for yourself. Congratulations. Most likely it includes most, if not all, of the following elements: a career, a family, personal interests, community, and a spiritual practice.

So how did you get everything you have? Again, I'll gamble a guess and suggest that you attribute your life achievements to taking action. You got an education. You got a job. You got a place to live. Many of you might have a partner or children. Cars, houses, or other material things that you own have come to you because you've taken action. You might be a volunteer, a coach, a mom, or a dad; you might love a pet, or have a hobby. Again, all of these are things that required action on your part. Think back on everything you have and everything you have done to date, and other than being a pretty impressive list, they all have one thing in common: You got off your butt and took action.

Physical activity is the literal version of getting off your butt and taking action. You have proof that a "take action" approach works—just look at your life. It is interesting how we can metaphorically move ourselves forward with gusto in our lives, but when it comes to literally moving ourselves forward, we prefer to stay seated working on emails.

Yes, your actions up to this point in your life have created a full life that, most likely, is just plain exhausting. The workdays get longer and longer, the kids' activities continue to grow, and your community involvement has evolved from volunteering your time to managing events. I know there have been many times when I have regretted all the action I took earlier in my life.

We've hit a point of diminishing returns. There are only so many emails/projects you can complete without burning out, or kids' functions you can attend before going insane. One more community event may have you wondering what it would be like to live on a deserted island for a while. We need an injection of energy, an outlet for stress, and time away from all of our successes. We need physical activity.

I'm purposefully using the term "physical activity." We see so much propaganda today—in the newspapers, on TV, on the Internet, or even just while talking to friends—about how we need to exercise more. The latest exercise craze has become almost as difficult to keep up with as the latest diet fad. We see pictures of gyms, treadmills, weights, and other exercise equipment paired with very attractive women and men, glistening with just enough sweat that they look as if they have been sprayed with morning dew. While many people enjoy exercising at a gym, a growing majority runs as quickly as possible the other way. Whether the issue is finding time to go, spending money to be subjected to pain, or feeling uncomfortable in our bodies or abilities, going to a gym just isn't for everyone.

Different from "exercise," physical activity can be done at any time, anywhere, in any style of clothing, and for no money. Physical activity can be fun, it can happen while spending valuable time with family or friends, it can occur during an important meeting with a client, it can take as little or as much time as you have to give, and, chances are, you are already doing more of it than you think you are. Add to the benefit list the fact that you will increase your energy, boost your creativity, better your mood, manage a healthy weight, look great, drink more water, be inclined to eat a healthier diet, sleep more, live longer, and set a healthy example for your colleagues and family. *That* is the power of physical activity.

So how do you find the time to get all of these benefits? You'll be surprised at how easy it is to get off your butt every day. For those of you who enjoy the gym experience, please, keep going. For those of you who get your exercise running away from the gym, here are some physical activity ideas to help you get your creative juices flowing:

- Golf with clients.
- Walk around your office space while on a conference call.
- Get up and stand in the back of the room during a presentation.
- Walk the long way to meetings.
- Take the stairs instead of the elevator.
- Plan a family hike/bike ride on the weekends, with picnic lunch.
- Walk after dinner with your partner and catch up on the day's events.

You can take these ideas even further to include:

- Have a "walking meeting"—go outside for a walk while discussing the latest project status.
- Do lunges and squats while on conference calls or, if it's a call where you are not speaking at regular intervals, take your phone for a walk outside (just ensure your phone is muted so you do not interrupt the meeting with birds singing, cars passing, or your own panting).
- Run the stairs at home during the commercials of your favorite television show or add a few sit-ups and push-ups during the next commercial break.

There are all sorts of ways to integrate physical activity into your already overloaded workday. Creativity, enjoyment, and setting yourself up for reasonable success are the keys to moving more. Moving more allows your mind to feed on much-needed oxygen and your body to be energized through the increased blood circulation. You will find that some fresh oxygen and increased blood circulation will do wonders for your creativity, problem-solving abilities, and overall mood.

For those of you who enjoy a regular exercise routine, keep it up. Ensure, like you do with your career and your family, that you are constantly finding new ways to elevate yourself and those around you. Set higher goals for yourself, and as you achieve them, notice the strength you gain, helping you to achieve more at work and play. You have figured out how to set your personal boundaries, allowing yourself time to train or exercise regularly. Now, apply the mental energy you gain through exercise to enhance other areas of your life. Yours is a different challenge, where the goal is less about finding time and more about channeling your energies to the highest levels you are able.

You have spent the majority of your life moving yourself forward. Use the lessons you've taught yourself up until now and move your *body* forward—and up and down, side-to-side, and 'round and 'round.

If you do nothing else: If you do not have a regular exercise routine, pick one new physical activity from the list above and plan to do it once this week. A walk/hike/bike ride with family members is a great place to start in your efforts—it's the biggest bang for your buck in the quest to live more, work better. If you do have a regular exercise routine, think about adding a regular walk/hike/bike ride with family members to your training—there is nothing healthier than spending time with loved ones and teaching them about good health.

Exploit Good Stress, Eliminate Bad Stress

Stress gets a bad rap. When asked how we are doing by our friends, colleagues, or family, if things are bad, we are quick to tell people we are "stressed-out," "stressing," or "under stress." Work is stressful, commuting to work is stressful, next weekend's family get-together will be stressful. Our foreheads crinkle up with stress lines and many of us experience stress headaches. And, of course, we all know that stress is a leading cause of heart attacks, strokes, and depression. Stressed, it seems, has become a synonym for tense, unhappy, and out of control.

But that's not what stress is actually about. Stress also rears its head when we're doing something adventurous for the first time, as the feelings of excitement and nervousness join forces. When we are in the middle of a great project at work, with our creative thinking hitting overdrive as we put all of our energies into delivering our best work on time, we are stressed. The feeling we get before we do a presentation that could result in a promotion? Stress. When we are training for a physical challenge and can't sleep the night before the big day, what's keeping us up? Stress. But these are all forms of *good* stress. When adrenaline is coursing through your body like a fire, your thoughts and abilities are heightened. You feel energized—yes, you are probably scared, nervous, and excited as well, but these feelings feed our ability to do more, create more, and be more.

Take a moment to reflect back on your life. What great things have you accomplished? Making a sports team, getting the lead in a school play, receiving the highest mark on an important test, getting into a great university—you had multiple victories even before you could drink. Getting your first job, your first promotion, your first raise. Finding your partner, having children, running a marathon, climbing a mountain. I'm sure there are many times in your life that you've felt success, so take a moment and remember how you felt: happy, elated, accomplished, euphoric, thrilled, like nothing could stop you.

Now take a moment and think about the days and actions leading up to each success. When I think about my pre-success times, I immediately relive the tensing in my stomach, the tingle in my fingers, and the increase in my heart rate that often kept me from breathing. My body was in a state of stress, but that stress prepared me to perform my best and reap the wonderful feelings of success afterward.

Another useful feature of good stress is its capacity to motivate you to get things done. When I first left the corporate world and started my own business, I got enormous amounts of advice from books, people, coaches, and of course, the Internet. One golden nugget in it all was to always book your presentation/meeting/speaking engagement *before* you have your material developed. The first time I heard this, I thought it was time to go back to my corporate job, as it was obvious to me that no one in the entrepreneurial world understood logic. But, as I looked more closely, I realized that hundreds of millionaires who are now coaching other people on how to make money doing what they love for a living must know something, right? And they all had the same advice, so they must have figured it out. Okay, I thought, I'd give it a try.

Within a month, I had the title and executive summary for a presentation I wanted to deliver to a group of young corporate executives being groomed for leadership positions. I pitched my idea and to my elated surprise, got the gig. I just had to figure out what detailed content to present. The presentation wasn't for another three weeks, so the first week I spent stressing about the fact that I only had three weeks to figure out how I was going to change the lives of ninety professionals. Week two was spent thinking of ideas and writing them down in a notepad in between answering unimportant emails and stalking Facebook. I spent many a sleepless night worrying about how I would be perceived, if people would like my work, and what I would wear. Finally, it was one week before my presentation—it was time to get serious.

The stress from weeks one and two were examples of bad stress anchored in worry and procrastination. It was when my deadline loomed in front of me so closely that I couldn't ignore it any longer that I finally sat down and started to write. Hours passed like minutes as my creative juices started to flow. Each idea I had became the nucleus of an intricate web of more and more brilliance. When cocktail hour arrived at the end of each day, instead of zoning out in front of the TV, I would take my wine to the other room and write more and more ideas down in my notebook. I got up early to get to work, nothing like my usual triple-snooze mornings with a bellyache of dread as to what the day might hold. That week passed with a sense of urgency wrapped so tightly in creative energy that I was exhausted and invigorated all at the same time when it was over. The good stress had carried me through to where I needed to be.

> ### *Good stress can do great things.*

Good stress accomplishes things. Bad stress wastes time and energy. So how do you exploit the good and eliminate the bad? First, set yourself up for success by doing the following:

1. As we have discussed, if you do not know—or are not constantly prioritizing—your life values (see Chapter Two), you will always have more bad stress than good stress in your life. This is simply because when you are in alignment with what you view as important and are channeling your energies into those people/ideals, the only stress you experience is the kind that moves you forward. Good stress will propel you through your fear of advancement and the unknown because you will know that you are headed in the right direction.

Bad stress only appears when you procrastinate or allow other people's priorities, urgencies, and values to replace yours. So take the time to identify what is important to you, what you love to do, and what you want to accomplish, then try as hard as you can to do more of those things.

2. Become an expert on noticing how bad stress impacts your body. The next time you are asked how you are and you answer "stressed out," take a quick inventory on how you feel (or listen closely to yourself as you tell someone else how unhappy you are). In fact, let's do a bit of work on that now. Turn to the back of the book and find the "**BAD STRESS/GOOD STRESS FEEL-INGS**" worksheet (or use a nearby notebook or piece of paper). Reflect for a moment on how you feel when you are "stressed out." Write down what you feel. How do you sound? What is your face doing? How does your belly feel? Are your shoulders hunched in? What about your outlook on life? Pessimistic? Whatever you notice, feel it in your body and write it down.

3. Now, do the same for when you feel good stress. Do you feel your adrenaline pumping through your body? Are you smiling? Do you tend to move faster? Is your mind clearer? Do you have a heightened sense of awareness? Are you happier? Energized? Whatever you notice, feel it in your body and write it down.

Being able to identify whether you are experiencing bad or good stress is the first step toward being able to reduce one and exploit the other.

WAYS TO ELIMINATE BAD STRESS

- **Stop overcommitting.** We create a lot of our own bad stress by agreeing to do things that we don't want to do, don't have to do, and—in many cases—shouldn't do. (If, at this point, you are still prone to overcommitting, I encourage you to return to and reread Chapter Three.)

- **Don't contribute to a "bad stress tornado."** A bad stress tornado is when one person, perhaps having a bad day, sends out an email or makes a comment in a meeting that is unhelpful, somewhat derogatory, lays blame on another individual, or is otherwise mean-spirited. Then, because others have either taken offense, are having a bad day themselves, are looking for a good fight, or are just mean-spirited themselves, they respond to the email ("reply to all"), or at the meeting, in a similar tone. It spirals out of control from there, each comment picking up more and more negative, mean-spirited comments simply because everyone has too much bad stress and they feel a need to let it all out. Eventually, the tornado will die out, but not before it demolishes the moods and productivity of everything (and everyone) in its path. When you see a "bad stress tornado" headed your direction, take cover, breathe deeply, keep your head down, do not get sucked in, and let it pass. You will stay safe, and you will avoid making the tornado worse. (This advice also works well when the "bad stress tornado" hits on the home front.)

- **Breathe.** Yes, just sit back, take a break, walk away, stop panicking, and take a long, deep breath. Start the breath in your lower abdomen (below your belly button) and pull it slowly through your body, up through your lungs, into your head. Now, hold it there for a second. OK, exhale. Slowly, like the inhale, take your time to let it all out. For even better effect, visualize your stress as the breath you take when you inhale.

For example, if a person is creating bad stress for you, picture them in you abdomen, moving through your body into your head, and then you exhale them out. They are gone. Out of your body. Let them go. You can do the same with a situation that is stressing you out. Visualize that situation as a ball of bad energy in your abdomen, breathe it deeply and slowly through your body, get it centered in your head, and then *whoosh*. Breathe it out. Let it go. Send it away.

HOW TO EXPLOIT GOOD STRESS:

- **Reward yourself for hitting both your personal and professional goals.** Remember when you were a child and each time you did well in school, you would receive a gold star from your teacher or a new toy you were coveting from your parents? Well, being an adult doesn't mean we shouldn't reward ourselves for a job well done. A massage, a vacation (maybe without kids), an afternoon golfing, a new electronic toy, or a new handbag. Whatever it is that makes you happy, do it for yourself after you have reached an aggressive life goal. This positive reinforcement will motivate you to reach more goals, thus creating an environment of continued good stress.

- **Approach work with a desire to make the world a better place—not just a need to get tasks done.** Most of us work because we have to, but many of us actually do enjoy the work that we do. But that enjoyment can get lost under layers of emails, meetings, conflicts, deadlines, and unbalanced bosses and colleagues. Before you drown in the bad stress of getting as many tasks done as possible in a day, stop for a moment and remember what you do enjoy about your career. Do you help people? Do you solve problems? Do you make things more efficient? What is the true essence of your job—the reason that you chose this profession to begin with?

- **Write down, preferably on another Post-it note, three things you enjoy about the work you do.** This is your "Reasons I Do This Job" list. Post that list someplace where you see it every day (I'd suggest directly on your computer). During the day, when you start to feel your body in "bad stress" mode, take that deep cleansing breath that we learned above, exhale whatever is causing you that "bad stress," then look at your list and remind yourself why you are there, doing your work. View the work you are doing through your "good stress" lens, and react to the email/client/colleague/boss in a constructive manner aligned with your "Reasons I Do This Job" list. If the task that is causing you stress is completely out of alignment with your "Reasons I Do This Job" list, then why not stop doing it? You can use tactics from the list below to eliminate it from your life.

If you do nothing else: Try the breathing exercise. Right now. See how it feels. There is nothing more cleansing than a deep breath.

Relax, Rejuvenate, and Renew

Relaxation, rejuvenation, and renewal (RRR) are not activities to be saved for vacation. They are to be practiced daily, weekly, monthly, and yearly, during your busiest times and your slowest times. The results of regular RRR practice can be a longer life, a more thoughtful approach to everyday life, and even fewer facial wrinkles. Like everything else in this chapter, the more you incorporate RRR into your daily health routine, the more balance you'll feel (and find) in your life.

For most of us, the idea of relaxing, rejuvenating, and renewing starts with a good night's sleep. And, for most of us, that good night's sleep is as elusive as winning the lottery, finding a pot of gold at the end of the rainbow, or discovering a deserted beach on a secluded island with a tiki bar just for you. A good night's sleep is something most of us have failed to have since we were kids, tucked under our covers with our only worry in the world being what would happen with our friends at school the next day. Deadlines, smartphones, children, stress, worry, never-ending "to do" lists, early-morning exercise sessions, late-night conference calls—there is no end to what erodes a good night's sleep. The incessant chatter in our heads rehashes the events of the day that just ended while preparing for the day to come. Sound sleep becomes wishful thinking.

Getting enough sleep is a necessity for your body and mind to work at their highest levels. Sure, you can *survive* on minimal sleep, but forget about ever thriving. You will stay suspended in a zone of constant exhaustion, always feeling as if you are hiking up one side of a mountain, and never getting a chance to slide down the other side. Studies show that getting seven to nine hours of sleep per night is optimal for most people; however, there are many people who need more than nine for top performance, and others who can produce amazing things with less than four. I used to work for a man whose productivity levels were off the charts, yet he never needed more than four hours of sleep every night. I knew that I would never live up to his example, nor did I want to. I personally believe that sleeping and eating are the best things in life, and love the fact that they can also be some of the healthiest.

There are a wealth of reports, studies, theories, and spiritual beliefs on what the process of sleeping does to your body and mind. What they all speak to is the fact that, while you are sleeping, your body and mind get a break, truly relax, and prepare themselves for another day. Sleeping is the most basic form of shutting yourself down for a period of time and allowing relaxation to occur; your body slows most of its processes—including breathing, heart rate, and even digestion—and your mind stops thinking, analyzing, and creating. Entering a truly relaxed state every night builds the resources you need to live in a more relaxed state during waking hours.

How can you get that elusive seven to nine hours of sleep every night? Here are some very practical recommendations that have worked for me and my clients:

- **Keep a pile of Post-it notes and a pen on your bedside table.** As you drift off to sleep only to be jolted upright by a thought of something you need to do the next day, lean over and write it down. Similarly, if you wake from a dead sleep in the middle of the night with an idea for the next day's ten o'clock meeting, lean over and write it down. How about the list of items you need to pack for little Mary's school outing the next day? You know what to do: Lean over and write it down. The act of getting things out of your head and onto a piece of paper will not only increase your productivity when you are awake, it will also allow you to stop thinking about things. Knowing that you will be able to remember what is on your mind will be immediately calming, quieting the useless chatter, list-building, and worry.

- **Breathe.** Take five to ten deep breaths, concentrating on each one from start to finish. Slowly inhale, bringing air into your lower lungs to a count of four, then exhale slowly, to another count of four, imagining the breath exiting your body with all the events that happened during your day. Repeat this process at least four times. As we did in the breathing exercise to reduce our "bad stress," gather each stressor up in a ball of energy you are inhaling through your body, then watch each of those stressors exit your body when you exhale. This process of focused breathing will help your mind enter a more relaxed state, thus allowing your body to follow. Similar to when you were a child and were told to count sheep to help you sleep, the process of focusing on something benign and breathing deeply will slow you down. By focusing your mind and calming your breath, you can put yourself into a wonderful state of relaxation.

- **Surround yourself with the right fragrances.** Get your hands on something that smells like lavender. This is a trick my mother used when we were kids, and—frankly—I thought she was a complete weirdo at the time. Now that I am an adult, I can say that my mother was right, and lavender has become one of my go-to solutions for relaxation—for myself and my clients. This is a form of aromatherapy—a type of alternative medicine that uses volatile plant materials, known as essential oils, and other aromatic compounds for the purpose of altering a person's mind, mood, cognitive function, or health. But don't let that scare you—it's basically just a fancy way of saying you're using a smell to elicit a response from your brain. Lavender, if inhaled, has been known to help ease exhaustion, insomnia, irritability, and even depression. You can get some lavender essential oil and, prior to turning out the light and hitting the pillow, rub a bit on your temples and a little in the opening of your nostrils (so you breathe in the essence longer). Or, you can get a lavender pillow and have it near your head. You can buy dried lavender wrapped in small bags and keep them under your pillow (this is especially good for traveling). There are so many alternatives for procuring lavender these days; find what you are comfortable with and try it out. Lavender essence, in conjunction with deep breathing, could be a great way to enhance your sleep.

- **Drink an herbal tea before bed.** Your local grocery store most likely has an extensive selection of "sleepy time" teas that have chamomile, lavender, valerian root, and other herbs known for inducing a relaxed state, allowing you to fall asleep. Instead of that last glass of wine, shot of espresso, or whatever your usual last beverage is, try replacing it with a cup of herbal tea. Herbal teas can make a wonderful accompaniment to your dinner's dessert, or can be sipped easily while reading a book or watching television. In fact, finding an herbal tea with mint in the mix will also help with digestion and could help eliminate any heartburn wake-up calls in the middle of the night.

- **Don't have that nightcap.** Avoiding alcohol for at least the hour before you retire to bed will make a significant difference in the quality and length of your sleep. Though a nightcap may help you relax and fall asleep faster, it will make the second half of your sleep cycle restless and unsatisfying, as alcohol decreases the amount of deep sleep you get and can increase the number of times you are aroused from your sleep. If you do plan to drink your alcohol with dinner, try a nice cup of herbal tea for dessert.

- **Do not work on emails (or any other work, if possible) after dinner.** In today's world of global, 24/7 work hours, I understand that virtual meetings may have to occur during what would be considered your normal sleeping hours and you don't always have control over their timing. But you have full control over when you do your own emails, and ending your day with a slew of stressed-out colleagues and clients is not conducive to a good night sleep. So don't subject yourself to them. As for the late-night or early-morning phone calls, limit them to no more than three per week. Others will understand you not being on a call at three o'clock in the morning. (And, seriously, how much value can one person add to a conversation at three o'clock in the morning?)

- **Charge your phone somewhere other than in your bedroom.** Do not leave your smartphone on the bed-side table next to you—it will beep, buzz, and otherwise distract you all night. Additionally, the electro-magnetic frequency emitted by our devices can mess with our bodies' natural electrical systems and circadian rhythms (including sleep cycle). Keeping smartphones out of sight, reach, and earshot will allow you to truly dis-connect from your day. Alarm clocks *did* exist prior to the smartphone, so saying that you need to use your smartphone as a replacement for an alarm clock is not a good enough reason to have it next to your bed all night. I'm sure you can still buy an alarm clock in your nearest department store. And, remember: In the spirit of not being plugged in, you do not need your smart-phone next to your bed to email yourself reminders for morning action. Post-it notes work just as well!

I think we would all agree: There is nothing like a good night's sleep to lift your mood, boost your energy level, increase your productivity, and make your physical appearance that much more attractive. Taking one hour from your late-night work commitments and giving it to your sleeping schedule will do wonders for your overall life balance.

Let's talk now about rejuvenation. Rejuvenation is the act of bringing something back to life. In this case, that something is you—and the best way to bring yourself back to life is to take a vacation.

For many of us, vacation means travelling to a destination where our days are spent living as if we were on an episode of *Lifestyles of the Rich and Famous*. Waking up without an alarm clock, watching the *Today* show instead of reading our emails, actually eating breakfast, then spending the day smiling, laughing, playing, and relaxing with the family. Early evening brings well-behaved children, cocktails, sunsets, dinners, and early bedtimes. We spend much of our time dreaming about how nice life would be if we lived the vacation life every day, and start to count the days until retirement offers us the freedom to truly live our lives. While on vacation, our bodies feel rested, fed, sun-kissed, and energized, our relationships with our families feel new and fun again, and we even feel slightly reinvigorated about getting back to work. That last part—reinvigorated about going back to work—usually appears because we once again feel in control, on top of our game, and able to get back to work with stronger boundaries, allowing the rejuvenation that occurred during vacation to seep into our "real" life.

Then, as much as we felt reborn from our vacation the first week back to work makes us feel exhausted again. So, how do we recharge ourselves on a regular basis and keep our batteries charged for longer than the first week back to work?

- **Take a two-week (or longer) vacation once a year.** You can do it. If you are worried about being away from work, reread Chapter Three. If you are worried about money or flexibility, stay home and take a "staycation." If you are worried about what others will think of your decision, go talk to a European professional. Europeans generally take extended vacations during the summer months to regenerate, and I'm sure any one of them would be happy to tell you, with disdain in their voice, that most people in the world take the vacation time allotted to them by their employers—and that if you don't, you have missed out on one of the best benefits of being employed. The point is not to worry about what you do or where you go, the point is about taking yourself out of the work environment for a total of two consecutive weeks and allowing yourself to rebuild, physically and mentally.

- **Don't "binge-work" when you get back.** The week you return to work from your vacation—or the day you return to work after a long weekend—restrain yourself from working more than an eight- to ten-hour day. I know, this is hard—emails have piled up, decisions need to be made, you need to catch up on what happened while you were gone, people need to talk to you, and your team needs your input to move forward—the demands on your time are endless. But remember: Everyone was able to manage without you while you were gone. There is no reason to get back to everyone during your first day/week back in the office. Take your time and be thoughtful about your workload. Don't answer email strings where you can see that decisions have already been made. Don't feel the need to catch up with everyone immediately—focus on those in your critical path (clients, bosses, and team members, in that order). Working until the wee hours of the morning your first day/week back to the office will immediately reverse the positive effects of your vacation. The life you were able to pump back into your body will be sucked back out and, worst of all, you will wonder if it will ever make sense for you to take time off again. Create your boundaries and *keep* your boundaries, because no one else will do that for you.

- **Drink more water and eat whole foods.** As we discussed earlier in this chapter, the benefits of drinking water and eating whole foods are numerous. In addition to what we've already discussed, drinking more water and eating whole foods rejuvenates your mind and body. Vitamins, minerals, and oxygen promote healthy cell growth, increase energy, promote restful sleep, and make you glow all over. Processed foods and sugary drinks stunt cell growth, decrease energy levels, give you heartburn at night, and result in many skin irritations and disease. Start eating and drinking better and you will rejuvenate your body from the inside out.

We've talked about relaxing and rejuvenating, let's now talk about renewing yourself. While the word "renew" may feel a bit daunting, in fact the process of bringing yourself back to "new" on a regular basis is the easiest of the three concepts. Renewing yourself is as easy as taking a breath.

While we've touched on breathing earlier, let's dive in a bit deeper. Yoga practitioners are familiar with the word *pranayama*, a Sanskrit word meaning "control of the life force." While many people relate deep breathing to yoga, meditation, or other forms of advanced healing and relaxation techniques, the reality is that deep breathing is something that can be done quickly and quietly, anytime and anywhere. After all, we breathe constantly, every minute of every day of every year that we're alive. We take our breath with us wherever we go. Breathing does not require a yoga mat or a meditation retreat. All it requires is a little acknowledgment and focus.

Stop reading for a moment and focus on your breath. You can breathe normally, or you can indulge yourself and take a really deep breath. Simply notice that the reason you are here is because you are still breathing. Think about how smart your body is that it knows to breathe in and out regularly to keep you alive. Remember what you learned in school about what is happening in your body when you breathe. Oxygen is being brought into your body through your nose or mouth, where it enters your lungs and feeds your blood stream, which in turn feeds your cells. On the exhale, carbon dioxide waste from your cells is sent back through the blood to the lungs, then out the nose and mouth. Your breath is the life-giving force to your body, which is pretty amazing if you stop and think about it.

When you breathe more deeply, focusing on an extended inhale and exhale, you not only allow for more oxygen to enter your body and more toxins to exit, you are also sending a signal to your brain that it's time to relax. This signal, once received in the brain, is then sent out to your entire physical body and you feel calmer immediately. This is the process of renewal—taking in new oxygen, getting rid of old toxins, and giving your mental and physical body a quick reboot from tension to relaxation.

Now, take that breath outside. Breathing in the fresh air that Mother Nature provides for us makes your renewal efforts that much more significant. Being in nature immediately makes us feel like new people. A walk in the woods (or park) is nice, but just being outside is what is important. In your back yard, on your deck, wherever you feel connected to the outdoor world around you, go there and take a few deep breaths. Smell the flowers. Enjoy the trees. Take your shoes off and feel your feet on the ground. Reconnect to the beautiful world around you, and you immediately feel revived. Even if you live in a cold area and it's wintertime and snowy, go outside and breathe in that crisp, clean air. Falling snow can be so exhilarating! If the spirit strikes you, stretch while you breathe. Bring your arms up over your head and give yourself a good stretch. Breathe deeply and, touching your hands to the ground (or at least reaching toward the ground), give your legs a good stretch. You can do this breathing and stretching renewal technique anywhere, but being in nature will enhance your results.

This process of stopping, breathing, and stretching will immediately change your outlook on whatever negative situation or thought is happening, and the best thing about this exercise is that you can do it anywhere, anytime, at no cost — and without anyone ever knowing.

If you do nothing else: Go to bed ten minutes earlier tonight than you did last night. Turn off the TV, shut your computer, put your smartphone out of reach, and get yourself into bed just ten minutes earlier than you did last night. Use that extra ten minutes to breathe deeply. Next week, add another ten minutes.

Remember, your body and your mind are at the center of your life balance scale. The stronger the scale's center, the less chance the scale has of tipping over when one side becomes heavier than the other. Over time, the attention you pay to your own body and mind will spill over into the attention you put into your entire life. This concept is actually a behavioral reality — how you do one thing is how you do everything. If you strive to keep yourself healthy, you will also then strive to keep your life healthy.

Keeping your body healthy = Keeping your life healthy

Chapter 5

Live a Life in Balance

We've done a lot of work together in a relatively short time. From understanding the source of our imbalances, to defining what "life balance" means on a personal level, to making small but powerful changes to our daily habits that encourage and support our desired state of being. We've climbed up the mountain, celebrated at the top, and are now ready to saunter down the other side into a life of balance.

That celebratory feeling of euphoria surrounds us as we breathe in the vision of how amazing our lives will be when every day is spent doing and having what we want, when and how we want it. We start to skip as the pure, childlike glee reminds us that we have nothing to fear; the whole world is our playground. *La la la, la la la, la la—BAM.*

We trip and fall over a stone and tumble gracelessly back into reality.

Too many times our best efforts and positive changes are derailed by "real life" stepping back in and taking over. In other words: Shit happens. But if you are prepared to deal with the imperfections, curveballs, and bad days, you will still remain balanced. Living a life in balance is about making forward progress every day—even when progress comes in the form of testing your willpower, your strength, and the strength of your desires. With consistent practice and support, your life will become, on a regular basis, the reality you created in Chapter Two.

Making Balance a Habit

According to the *Webster's New World Dictionary*, a habit is "a thing done often and hence, usually done easily." Habits can range from rushing your teeth, reading a book before bed, stopping for coffee on your way to the office, to having pizza every Friday night.

Think for a moment about the good habits in your life. I'm pretty sure that you have activities that you do every day to make your life better.

Balance is just another item that you can incorporate into your life in a regular and repeated way. You have created other habits in your life and there is no reason why you can't choose to make balance a habit as well. All you really need to do is make the decision to take action. Then, keep making that same decision to take action over and over until you are no longer making a decision to do something, you are just doing it because that's what you do.

The more your life falls into the balance you crave, the easier it will be to make good decisions, keep your boundaries, pay attention to your health, and be acutely aware of when the outside world is robbing you of your power. To put it bluntly: The more you are in balance, the easier it is to maintain balance.

> *It's all about inertia: The more you are in balance, the easier you can maintain balance.*

Once you have created a habit of balance, you will see the matrix for what it really is: other people who have yet to figure out their own life balance and are scared to do things differently. There are more of them than there are of you, so it's sometimes hard to maintain a way of life that isn't the norm.

We are all constantly surrounded by workaholics, perfectionists, performance addicts, and overachievers, so those of us who have found balance are an endangered minority. It's hard to be in the minority, constantly standing up for yourself and your values when the majority sees things differently. But if you keep with it, you will be feeling so good about yourself and your life that it won't matter. You won't want this feeling called "balance" to escape you ever again. So, fight the good fight, stick to your values and principles, and slowly you will see that not only are your habits changing you for the better, but that you also have the power to change and help those around you.

> **Make balance a habit by implementing one action at a time.**

The easiest way to make balance a habit is to pick one action to implement at a time. Successfully implement that action, then add another. Move slowly but methodically. Consistent baby steps forward are always better than running too fast, which can set you up for trips and falls. Many people fail to create good habits because they jump headfirst into a new idea, process, or way of doing something and—within a few weeks—burn out. We are programmed to try to do everything perfectly—and quickly. Balance is not perfect, and it most definitely does not come quickly, so appreciate those facts and move at a pace conducive to long-term change.

Start with identifying one item from Chapter Three that will reduce the amount of time you spend working every day, and do that regularly until it becomes second nature to you. For example, start with your vanishing "to do" list. You will need a few weeks, at least, to get good at this exercise, so you'll have to stick to it for a bit to see results.

At the same time, also pick one easy item from Chapter Four to incorporate into your daily routine. How about drinking more water? Try my trick where you keep a glass of water on your bedside table and then you drink the entire glass in the morning before you are dressed. It's easy enough to do and, after a few weeks, not only will it become second nature to you, you will feel so energized by the water that you will look forward to that glass every morning. As easy as that, a habit is born.

What you pick to do is up to you, just remember: It takes time to create a habit. So move slowly. Pick easy actions first so your chances of success increase. The more success you have, the more success you will crave.

You have a long life ahead of you—take your time and make lasting changes.

> *If you do nothing else:* Pick your two items (one from Chapter Three, one from Chapter Four) and commit to incorporating them into your daily routine starting right now.

Redefining Happiness and Abundance

Remember that promotion I didn't get? Besides feeling like a failure, I also felt as if I would never be happy or have the abundance I desired in my life. I had tied my happiness so tightly to my promotion that when I didn't get the promotion, I felt as if I'd never achieve happiness. Taking my life back on my own terms was one step to reclaiming my true happiness; but, in fact, it was something deeper that lead to my ultimate redefinition of happiness.

During an alcohol-induced debrief with my husband about my non-promotion unhappiness, he asked me: "What will make you happy?" I took a few minutes to think about the question; then I realized that happiness for me didn't mean a promotion—happiness meant freedom. Freedom to do what I wanted, when I wanted, and how I wanted. Happiness meant exploring our natural world and appreciating its beauty and history. Happiness meant getting up in the morning and looking forward to whatever my schedule held—both professionally and personally. Happiness meant having enough money to live a comfortable life, travel, and wine and dine well. Ironic moment—I realized that my life was far from happy. With the exception of making a lot of money, I wasn't well aligned on any of the other items on my happiness list.

So we made a pact to start focusing on our happiness. Exactly nineteen months later (seven months after I was eventually promoted), we left our jobs, put most of our lives in storage, and backpacked around the world for a year. That year of exploring our capacity for happiness led to an amazing job for me when we returned—one that I would not have applied for had I not taken a year off. When you make yourself happy, the world around you conspires to support that happiness, long term.

What truly makes *you* happy? What are your core desires? How would you really like to live your life if you didn't have to worry about money, status, or what other people think?

Here's the perfect opportunity for you to take a few minutes and reflect on the questions above. I've added a blank page entitled "**WHAT MAKES ME HAPPY?**" at the end of the book for you to use to capture your thoughts (or—you know the drill—if you're reading this as an e-book, just find a blank piece of paper or some Post-it notes). Don't allow any judgment to enter your mind as you write. Hey, if making loads of money makes you happy, then write it down! If looking good makes you happy, be proud that you can articulate what makes you happy and write it down. You can use your "Who Am I?" and "Who Do I Want to Be?" lists to brainstorm ideas if needed.

Understanding what truly makes people happy is central to the coaching work I do with my clients—it's the essence of living your life in balance. Once we understand what truly makes us happy—and we are able to see the abundance that flows from that place—life becomes balanced.

> *Where happiness goes, abundance will follow.*

Abundance follows happiness. During my darker days (prior to my no promotion turning point), I equated abundance to money and things. After my enlightenment, I realized that abundance is not about having a lot of money, it's about having a fulfilling life filled with happiness. But, because I am a practical realist, I will confirm that happiness *won't* buy a nice bottle of Chardonnay. Unless, of course, you are happy about the work that you do; in that case, happiness might buy that bottle of Chardonnay, with enough funding left over for the scallops over spinach salad. Why? Because when you do what makes you happy, you work harder, smarter, and better, which ultimately creates all the abundance you need—professionally and personally.

The next time you find yourself saying, "How could I? It's not possible. I'll never make enough money. I'd really love to X, Y, Z, but just can't right now," or any variation of those, stop yourself. Instead, ask yourself: "Why not me? Why can't I? What's holding me back?" and "What am I scared of?"

Sometimes there are real hurdles that need to be dealt with, but, most of the time, we are just scared. Scared to do what really makes us happy because we will risk the "safety" of what we have. A need for safety is understandable, but often shortsighted.

There are so many ways to live your life. Choosing to live your life scared will not get you many places. Choosing to live your life in balance means that you will spend your days doing what makes you happy and brings you the abundance you desire.

It's up to you to take the time to understand what happiness and abundance really mean to you, then pursue those things with faithful abandonment. Once you find out what is important, getting to that goal may mean big changes to your current life — or maybe even just small modifications — but the sooner you engage yourself in choosing your own path, the sooner you will be able to live the rest of your life in balance.

> *If you do nothing else:* Find one word to describe one thing that makes you happy and say it out loud. Sometimes just talking about happiness makes you happy.

Just Do It

If you have made it through this book, chances are good that you see a lot of yourself in me — a recovering perfectionist with workaholic tendencies. One characteristic of a recovering perfectionist with workaholic tendencies is that you tend to believe that if you want something done right, you'll have to do it yourself.

You love a good challenge, usually bite off more than you really want to chew, and feel responsible for other people's problems and successes. You are a good person, you care, you want to do well, provide, and thrive. Here, in these qualities, lies the strength you need to live more and work better.

Channel your brilliance, determination, wisdom, and desire into yourself — and be amazed by the result. Create a work plan for your own life balance and use your "get it done" mentality to make it happen. Nobody is going to create a plan for you.

If you have an ideal of what your life should be, go get it. You have the power to live a balanced life—so just do it.

Remember the words of wisdom from Bon Jovi's song "It's My Life":

It's my life
It's now or never
I ain't gonna live forever
I just want to live while I'm alive
(It's my life)

It's *your* life. Figure out who you are. Define who you want to be. Create your own reality. Build a healthy body and mind. And the impossible will become possible—a life in balance.

If you do nothing else: Enjoy life, live life, be happy, and, if you liked this book, recommend it to your friends, family, and coworkers. The more you enlighten the people around you, the easier it will be to live more and work smarter—because everyone will be doing it!

Appendix

Working Papers

As you read through this book, you'll be asked at different times to do some written work. Use the following pages to do it. It might not be quite as colorful as my notebook stuffed with Post-it notes, but it will probably be easier to keep in one place.

(Oh, and don't feel bad about marking up the book. I don't mind.)

Who Am I?

WHO DO I WANT TO BE?

FANTASY DAY

MY WHYS AND MY WHATS

WANT "TO DO" LIST

FUTURE "TO DO" LIST

LEFTOVER "TO DO" LIST

WHY DO I DO WHAT I DO?

BAD STRESS/GOOD STRESS FEELINGS

WHAT MAKES ME HAPPY?